THE GOLDEN RULES

Competition can bring many benefits – or so all the politicians say. Bridge players certainly subscribe to such a theory. These days somewhere between two thirds and three quarters of all auctions see both sides entering the fray. Having a basic knowledge of how to get into or stay in the bidding is thus a key attribute for success at the bridge table.

You will often hear rules quoted such as 'do not double them into game' or 'leave the five level to the enemy'. This book covers all the rules likely to help you and, as usual in this series, you will find plenty of examples both for and against each one.

Marc Smith has a special interest in bidding. He has written regular articles on bidding theory, hosts *Bridge Magazine's* 'Partnership Profile' and provides a bidding quiz in *Bridge Plus*. His earlier writings on the subject have won coveted awards, and he has conducted an Internet bidding panel competition for *Bridge-Forum*. Julian Pottage needs little introduction either. He, too, has a monthly column in both the UK magazines, and the number of his books runs into double figures.

Players of all levels should gain something from reading these pages. As the authors deal with the groundwork, they add little jewels of advice along the way that will doubtless appeal to the higher echelons. Armed with the information in this book, you need never feel unprepared for when one of your opponents comes into the bidding.

by Julian Pottage and Marc Smith
THE GOLDEN RULES OF DEFENCE
THE GOLDEN RULES OF DECLARER PLAY
THE GOLDEN RULES OF CONSTRUCTIVE BIDDING

by Julian Pottage
MASTERPIECES OF DECLARER PLAY
MASTERPIECES OF DEFENCE

THE GOLDEN RULES OF COMPETITIVE AUCTIONS

Julian Pottage
and
Marc Smith

CASSELL
IN ASSOCIATION WITH
PETER CRAWLEY

First published in Great Britain 2003
in association with Peter Crawley
by Cassell
Wellington House, 125 Strand, London WC2R 0BB
an imprint of the Orion Publishing Group Ltd

The right of Julian Pottage and Marc Smith
to be identified as authors of this book
has been asserted by them in accordance with
the Copyright, Designs and Patents Act 1988

A catalogue record for this book is available
from the British Library

ISBN 0-304-36585-8

Printed and Bound in Great Britain by
Clays Ltd, St Ives plc

Contents

		page
	Foreword	7
1.	Overcall	9
2.	Compete when Short in Their Suit	19
3.	Compete via a Double	29
4.	Cue-Bid the Enemy Suit	45
5.	Pre-empt to the Limit	58
6.	Tread Warily after Their Pre-empt	67
7.	Be Cautious in Save Situations	77
8.	Double Opposing Sacrifices	86
9.	When in Doubt, Bid One More	94
10.	Leave the Five Level to the Enemy	105
11.	Do Not Double Them into Game	112
12.	Beware of Free Doubles	123
13.	Pass Partner's Penalty Doubles	138
14.	Stand Opponent's Doubles	146
15.	Never Redouble	152

Acknowledgments

The authors would like to thank the proof-reading team who for this book comprised: Graham Allan, Peter Burrows and Maureen Dennison. Their eagle eyes and red pens brought an extra dimension to a number of the key points.

We are also grateful to our family, friends and colleagues for their assistance, moral or otherwise, in enabling us to complete the work.

Foreword

Today's bridge world is an increasingly competitive one. These days you can rarely enjoy a free run to the best spot. Opponents come in at every turn, and often with a pre-emptive bid that takes several rounds of bidding away. Conventions and correct evaluation technique help to solve such problems but underlying these are the golden rules.

No matter whether your usual form of playing is at rubber, pairs, teams or Chicago the golden rules assist you in coming to the winning decision. In our examples we have tried to confine the bidding methods to those with which most people are familiar, but we have mentioned special treatments that work on certain types of hand. In the auctions we have used an asterisk to denote a bid that would be alerted at the table. An alert tells you that the bid does not mean quite what it says. It might show a different suit (a transfer maybe) or simply a weak hand (say, a Weak Two opener) or ask a specific question (4NT Blackwood or RKCB). As in the companion book *The Golden Rules of Constructive Bidding* you take the West seat throughout.

Even the best of players can find high level bidding decisions tricky. The stakes can be high if both sides can make game or someone is in danger of conceding a big penalty. There can be few things worse than losing 500 when you could have collected the same amount. Likewise everyone hates to get on the wrong end of a double game swing. Whilst we cannot guarantee that reading this book will enable you always to choose the winning action, it should undoubtedly point you in the right direction. Whether you play for master points, money, or just for fun we wish you success for the future!

Julian Pottage
Marc Smith

January 2003

[BLANK]

Rule One: Overcall

In the early days of contract bridge, the opening side had things pretty much their own way. It was tacitly assumed that whoever spoke first would own the hand. Even in the quite recent past, one would hear an overcall described as 'butting in'.

In fact, you can often make a contract after your opponents have opened the bidding: commonly a part-score, sometimes a game and occasionally a slam. When you have nothing on, there are still a multitude of reasons for wanting to join in the bidding – to make life difficult for the enemy, to direct a lead, or to find a paying sacrifice, for example. We start with some of the most common cases for sticking in your oar.

	♠ K 10 4		♠ 7 3
	♡ A Q 10 7 4 2		♡ K 9 6 5
	◇ K 3		◇ A Q J 5
	♣ 8 2		♣ J 6 4

YOU	LHO	PARTNER	RHO
–	–	–	1♠
2♡	Pass	4♡	

The opening bid on your right does not preclude you from being the pair with the easy game available. Here, it just so happens that the opponent who was first to speak holds the majority of his side's values. Indeed, it is the opening bid that makes Four Hearts so likely to succeed since the opener rates to hold the ♠A. Even if your game is in theory destined to go down, your LHO (left-hand opponent) will frequently lead a spade from a holding such as A-x after his partner's opening bid.

In this case, opener has laid claim to the master suit. Despite this, depending on the vulnerability, Four Spades may prove an expensive save for your opponents.

Note that we have shown partner raising directly to game, as he would at the rubber bridge table. In tournament play he may prefer to make a cue bid, a subject we will cover later.

```
        ♠ K 6            ♠ J 10 4 2
        ♡ 7 2            ♡ K 10 6 3
        ◇ A 9 3          ◇ K J 4
        ♣ K Q 10 7 6 4   ♣ A J
```

YOU	LHO	PARTNER	RHO
–	–	–	1♡
2♣	Pass	3NT	

Your side can certainly have game available in no-trumps after an opponent's opening bid. This applies particularly when your long suit is a minor as you may not have enough for an 11-trick game.

Expecting a reasonable 6-card suit and a smattering of high cards for your 2-level overcall, partner has an easy 3NT bid. ***Overcalling can help you reach your own best contract***.

♠ Q 10 8 7 4	YOU	LHO	PARTNER	RHO
♡ K 6	–	–	–	1♣
◇ 6 4	?			
♣ K J 7 5				

This time you have only 9 HCP and a distinctly moderate suit. There is no reason for you to expect this deal to belong to your side, but this hardly means you should remain silent.

Taking up the opponents' bidding space will often force them to guess and they will sometimes misjudge. Entering with a One Spade overcall prevents your LHO from making a simple response in either red suit, and he may lack the strength or the right shape to bid at the 2-level.

Your overcall also gives partner a number of options. With a good hand and three spades, he should be able to contest the part-score effectively, something he might only do when he knows about your probable 5-card suit. With a weaker hand but at least four spades he can pre-empt – perhaps finding a profitable sacrifice, or at least making life very tough for opener. Of course, your partner needs to be on the same wavelength and not blithely assume you possess the values for an opening bid. When you make a bid that cuts out the opposing bidding space, he must allow for this sort of hand.

♠ 6 3	YOU	LHO	PARTNER	RHO
♡ 7 4	–	–	–	1♣
◊ Q J 10 9 7 4	?			
♣ A K 8				

Overcalling One Diamond will scarcely trouble LHO since he can still bid either major at the 1-level. Even so, a One Diamond overcall should work much better than a pass – it may enable partner to compete or pre-empt, or it may direct him to the winning lead.

Still better, if your system allows it, is a jump overcall to Two Diamonds. You remove a whole level of the opponents' bidding space whilst telling partner about your promising 6-card suit and your approximate strength. *Overcalling can obstruct the opposition*.

♠ K J 10 9 5	YOU	LHO	PARTNER	RHO
♡ A 2	–	–	–	1◊
◊ Q 4 2	?			
♣ 8 6 2				

As mentioned above, an overcall can yield lead-directing benefits. If LHO becomes declarer, in a heart or a no-trump contract perhaps, the odds are that a spade lead will help your side. If you pass over One Diamond, the chance that partner will find the winning lead from a holding like ♠8-6-2 or ♠Q-4 falls significantly.

♠ 7	YOU	LHO	PARTNER	RHO
♡ A K Q 2	–	–	Pass	1♣
◊ 10 8 6 4	?			
♣ Q 10 5 3				

You will generally hold a 5-card suit when you overcall, but even that 'rule' can be broken sometimes because of the lead-directing benefits that may arise. Facing a passed partner, it appears unlikely that this deal belongs to your side. Moreover, your singleton spade suggests where their best fit lies, and it seems virtually certain that LHO intends to introduce that suit at his first turn.

A heart lead figures to be best for your team, and this looks like your last chance to make it easy for partner to find. *Overcalling can direct the lead*.

	YOU	LHO	PARTNER	RHO
♠ A 10 7 6 4	YOU	LHO	Pass	1♡
♡ 8 6 3	–	–	Pass	1♡
◊ K Q 10 6	?			
♣ 4				

Once again, partner's pass strongly suggests the deal belongs to the opponents. Holding the master suit may enable you to outbid the enemy, though. Picture partner with something like this:

♠ K 9 5 3 2   ♡ J   ◊ J 8 5 3   ♣ 9 6 2

Do you want to defend? The opponents can make at least eleven tricks in either hearts or clubs (twelve if their diamonds are 4-1 or their spades 3-0). You can also make a fair number of spades and a sacrifice should prove much cheaper than defending. Still, you can hardly expect partner to enter the auction off his own bat whatever the level . . . *Overcalling can let you find a good sacrifice*.

♠ A J 4	♠ K Q 10 9 6
♡ Q 5	♡ K 7 4
◊ A K 10 7 5	◊ Q 8 6
♣ 9 4 2	♣ 7 3

YOU	LHO	PARTNER	RHO
–	–	–	1♣
1◊	Pass	1♠	Pass
2♣	Pass	2◊	Pass
2♠	Pass	4♠	

When you overcall, you are normally telling partner that you have some values and are indicating where they may lie. With these two hands Four Spades will make easily, but suppose RHO had passed and you had opened with a weak (12-14) no-trump. With 10 HCP and a flattish hand, partner would do well merely to try for game.

In this auction, partner's hand improves by knowing his diamond holding faces a decent 5-card suit. The ◊Q has grown in stature and becomes worth much more than the normal 2 HCP. So, when you cue-bid to show a strong hand and then support his suit, partner can go to game. *Overcalling can show where your strength lies*.

♠ K Q 10 6 5	YOU	LHO	PARTNER	RHO
♡ K J 8 7 5	–	–	–	1◇
◇ 6 2	?			
♣ 3				

One option is to start by bidding your spades with the intention of bidding, and perhaps rebidding, hearts later. However, this strategy may prove unworkable in a competitive auction. The bidding may have reached an uncomfortably high level by the time you get to speak a second time. Suppose the auction were to continue:

YOU	LHO	PARTNER	RHO
–	–	–	1◇
1♠	2♣	Pass	3♣
?			

Vulnerable, would you feel happy about bidding Three Hearts?

Thankfully, we can give an easy way to avoid this predicament, and that is by overcalling in *both* of your suits at your first turn.

YOU	LHO	PARTNER	RHO
–	–	–	1◇
2◇			

This is called a 'Michaels Cue bid' – an immediate cue bid of RHO's minor-suit opening shows at least 5-5 in the majors. (If they open one of the majors then, using Michaels, a cue bid shows the other major and an undefined minor.)

Other methods for overcalling on two-suited hands do exist, but Michaels is the easiest and the most popular.

♠ 4	YOU	LHO	PARTNER	RHO
♡ 6	–	–	–	1♠
◇ K 9 6 4 2	2NT			
♣ A Q 10 7 5 3				

A similar method allows you to show both minors (after a major-suit opening from RHO). This is universally known as the 'Unusual No-trump'. ***Overcalling can allow you to bid two suits at once.***

	YOU	LHO	PARTNER	RHO
♠ 7 3	YOU	LHO	PARTNER	RHO
♡ K 4	–	–	–	1♣
◇ A K 9 6 5	1◇			
♣ Q 10 7 3				

With moderate hands, like the one here, you need to get into the auction as soon as possible, while the bidding remains at a low level. Suppose you were to pass RHO's One Club opening. The auction may continue:

YOU	LHO	PARTNER	RHO
–	–	–	1♣
Pass	1♡	Pass	1♠
Pass	2♠	Pass	Pass
?			

Do you feel happy about defending? The opponents have found a fit, yet not tried for game. They may very well make their contract, but generally they will own little more than half the high cards when they stop at the 2-level. It seems quite possible that the deal belongs to your side in a diamond part-score. In any case, you would rather defend against 3♠ than 2♠.

So, are you now going to come in with Three Diamonds? Doing so may prove effective since partner could have a 4-card diamond fit with you. It could also backfire quite badly – partner holding a 3-5-1-4 shape, for instance.

If you had come in immediately over RHO's One Club, you would have avoided facing this dilemma. *Overcalling can get you into the bidding at a safe level.*

During the late 1970s and early 1980s, strong club systems were highly popular in tournament play. No doubt, the recurring success of the Italian Blue Team at World Championship level had something to do with this. Indeed, few today would disagree with the contention that, in an uncontested auction, a pair using a strong club system has an edge over people using natural methods. Quite simply, if left to their own devices, a strong pair is highly likely to reach the best contract on game and slam deals. This makes it important that you put a spoke in their wheels whenever you get half a chance.

♠ K J 6 4 3	YOU	LHO	PARTNER	RHO
♡ 8	–	–	–	1♣ *
◇ 7 6 5	?			
♣ Q 10 7 5				

Having concluded that your strong club opponents will reach the right contract if left alone, logic dictates that you should try to interfere with their auction whenever possible. Indeed, one school of thought believes you should always come in over a strong club opening when you hold a bad hand, certainly when non-vulnerable.

Clearly, a One Spade overcall can be considered 'middle-of-the-road' on the hand above. Some might consider it too pedestrian, and prefer a jump overcall of Two Spades at the right vulnerability. If you are armed with a conventional counter, you might also have the option of a jump to Two Hearts (indicating either length in hearts or a 3-suited hand with short hearts) or perhaps a gadget that covers two odd suits or a major/minor two-suiter. There are many weird and wonderful methods on the market for defending against a strong club. That you act, rather than tamely passing, is probably more important than what you actually bid. *Overcalling can derail the opponent's system*.

♠ 10 7 6 5 2	YOU	LHO	PARTNER	RHO
♡ K Q J 5	–	–	Pass	1♡
◇ J 6	?			
♣ K 6				

You can take a good thing too far, and a One Spade overcall on this collection would be doing just that. This hand gives you two obvious reasons for remaining silent: you have a bad suit that you do not want partner to lead, and bidding One Spade over One Heart will hardly inconvenience the opponents because it uses up no real space.

There is also a third reason for passing – your values are all defensive in nature. With such a poor hand for offensive purposes, you hardly want partner pre-empting. Even worse, do you really want to encourage him to sacrifice in Four Spades when the opponents get to Four Hearts? To overcall on a suit as bad as this you would need the values for an opening bid and even then you would want to look for an alternative.

♠ K J 6	YOU	LHO	PARTNER	RHO
♡ A 8 2	–	1♡	Pass	1♠
◇ K 4	?			
♣ K 10 9 6 5				

A 2-level overcall will usually deliver a decent 6-card suit. In the 'sandwich seat' or 'dangerous position' (i.e., in fourth chair after an opening bid and change-of-suit response), which makes it relatively easy for the opponents to double you for penalties, the need to hold a respectable suit assumes even more importance than usual.

Not only does this hand lack a good enough suit for a Two Club overcall, but it also contains strong defensive values. This means that finding partner with a reasonable club fit may yet produce a bad score. For example, you might still fare poorly going one down in Three Clubs if it turns out that the opponents would have failed in their 2-level major-suit contract. ***Do not overcall when your values are defensive in nature***.

An element of danger attaches to any action, but the risk involved with bidding can outweigh the potential reward . . .

♠ Q J	YOU	LHO	PARTNER	RHO
♡ 9 6 5	–	–	–	1♡
◇ A Q 4 3 2	?			
♣ Q J 7				

A Two Diamond overcall seems most unwise here for several reasons. Your suit lacks texture and you have no sure winners outside – if the final contract becomes Two Diamonds Doubled, it could get bloody. Even if you buy the contract undoubled, particularly if partner makes a defensive raise, you figure to lose out when you hold defensive values that prevent the opponents from making a contract. Another route to a poor result after an overcall could come if partner, expecting a better hand and suit from you, carries the bidding too high.

♠ A K 5	YOU	LHO	PARTNER	RHO
♡ A 9 3	–	–	Pass	1♠
◇ Q 8 6 2	?			
♣ Q 7 4				

You hold the shape, the point count (just) and the spade stoppers for a 1NT overcall, but your playing strength is minimal. Facing a hand that could not open, the chance that passing now will result in a missed game if partner holds most of the outstanding high cards appears remote. Equally, when the bulk of the strength is with your LHO, he will have an easy double of your 1NT overcall. If this happens, then facing a dummy virtually devoid of high cards, you may end up making no more than your three obvious winners. ***Do not overcall when you might concede a large penalty***.

	YOU	LHO	PARTNER	RHO
♠ J 7 6 5 2	YOU	LHO	PARTNER	RHO
♡ A Q 10 4	–	–	–	1♣
◇ Q 6	?			
♣ J 3				

Yes, you have a 5-card major and a few values, but do you really want to overcall One Spade on this miserable collection? Doing so will sometimes work out right but, with such poor offensive values, it will often turn a plus into a minus when partner competes. An added disadvantage may arise if your LHO becomes declarer, perhaps in a no-trump contract. Are you sure you want partner to lead a spade? Doing so from ♠A-x, ♠K-x or ♠Q-x could easily cost a trick, and from two small cards it will surrender a tempo.

If you remain silent, you should be happy whatever partner leads. ***Do not overcall when you want partner to lead another suit***.

	YOU	LHO	PARTNER	RHO
♠ Q 7 5	YOU	LHO	PARTNER	RHO
♡ A 10 7 6 3	–	–	Pass	1◇
◇ Q 6 2	?			
♣ Q 4				

Facing a passed partner, you stand little real hope of buying the contract. Nor do you especially desire a heart lead if LHO becomes declarer. On this hand, you have an added reason to keep quiet. Your hand includes three queens, and there seems a chance that an opposing declarer will have a two-way finesse against at least one. Your overcall may provide the only clue about which defender has some strength. It could be just what he needs. ***Do not overcall when bidding is most likely to help an opposing declarer***.

♠ K 10 7 6 5	YOU	LHO	PARTNER	RHO
♡ 6 3	–	1NT	Pass	2◇ *
◇ A J 8	Pass	2♡	Pass	Pass
♣ Q J 4	2♠			

RHO's transfer bid showing hearts gives you two ways to make a Two Spade overcall. You can follow the auction above or you can come in at your first turn. Logic dictates that bidding immediately, before the opponents have limited themselves by attempting to stop at the 2-level, should show the better hand.

In the auction shown here, partner knows you have bid his values as well as your own, so there is no danger he will carry you too high or over-compete. ***Do not overcall when a delayed action better expresses your marginal values.***

Golden Rule One:

Overcalling can

. . . Help you reach your own best contract;
. . . Obstruct the opposition;
. . . Direct the lead;
. . . Let you a find a good sacrifice;
. . . Show where your strength lies;
. . . Allow you to bid two suits at once;
. . . Get you into the bidding at a safe level;
. . . Derail the opponents' system.

Do not Overcall when

. . . Your values are defensive in nature;
. . . You might concede a large penalty;
. . . You want partner to lead something else;
. . . Bidding is most likely to help an opposing declarer;
. . . A delayed action better expresses your marginal values.

Rule Two: Compete When Short in Their Suit

Times are rare when power alone allows you to compete effectively. In most cases, you also need a fit. The fewer cards you hold in the opponents' long suit, the greater the chance your side will have a decent fit. Consider the mathematics: if they own an 8-card fit, you will too unless your side's cards divide 7-7-7-5 between the suits. When they hold a 9-card fit, you must hold an 8-card fit (or better).

You will often have to pass an opposing bid holding fair values in a flat hand. So the onus falls on the player with the shapely hand, and the shortage in the opposing suit, to get his side into the auction.

East–West game
Dealer South

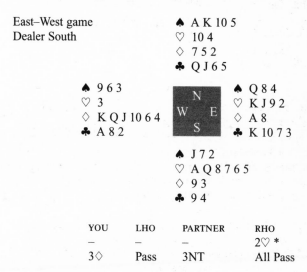

	♠ A K 10 5
	♡ 10 4
	♢ 7 5 2
	♣ Q J 6 5

♠ 9 6 3		♠ Q 8 4
♡ 3	N	♡ K J 9 2
♢ K Q J 10 6 4	W E	♢ A 8
♣ A 8 2	S	♣ K 10 7 3

	♠ J 7 2
	♡ A Q 8 7 6 5
	♢ 9 3
	♣ 9 4

YOU	LHO	PARTNER	RHO
–	–	–	2♡ *
3♢	Pass	3NT	All Pass

Holding only 10 HCP, coming in at the 3-level over the Weak Two might seem risky, but so is crossing the street.

What can partner do if you pass Two Hearts around to him? For a start, he has what look like wasted high cards in opener's suit. With no long suit, the wrong shape for a takeout double, and a hand too weak to reopen with 2NT, he will surely pass. As a result, you miss a vulnerable game. Since you hold the shortage in opener's suit, it is your job to get the partnership into the auction. ***Competing when short in their suit can help you find your own best contract.***

Love All ♠ 7 4
Dealer South ♡ K J 6 5
  ◇ Q 8 7 3
  ♣ J 9 4

♠ A Q 6 5 ♠ K 10 8 2
♡ 4 ♡ Q 10 3
◇ K 10 6 2 ◇ A 9 4
♣ 8 6 5 2 ♣ Q 7 3

  ♠ J 9 3
  ♡ A 9 8 7 2
  ◇ J 5
  ♣ A K 10

YOU	LHO	PARTNER	RHO
–	–	–	1♡
Pass	2♡	Pass	Pass
?			

Expert circles regard Love All (neither side vulnerable) as 'bidder's vulnerability' because it offers all four players the best conditions to contest a part-score. If either side goes down, it is only at 50 a trick (unless someone doubles). Indeed, in these circumstances, you could almost have scraped up a takeout double of One Heart.

Once the opponents find a fit, you can almost guarantee that one side or other (perhaps both) can make a part-score at the 2-level. It cannot, therefore, be right to defend Two Hearts – if you can make Two Spades, you have to get there; if they can make Two Hearts, Two Spades will prove a cheap save should it go one down. On this West hand, you should reopen the auction with a takeout double when Two Hearts comes round to you at any score.

Bidding like this carries little danger since you can tell that your side will hold close to 20 HCP because the opponents have settled at the 2-level despite agreeing a suit. Partner should not carry you overboard because he ought to know that you have already bid his values for him. He should only bid on with wild shape. If LHO takes the push to Three Hearts, partner should pass. The handy result for your side is 3♡ down one instead of 2♡ making. *Competing when short in their suit can push your opponents up a level.*

Game All

Dealer West

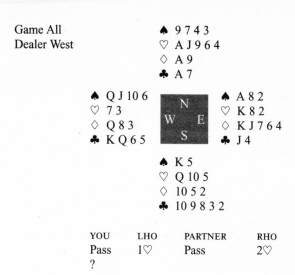

```
                    ♠ 9 7 4 3
                    ♡ A J 9 6 4
                    ◇ A 9
                    ♣ A 7
  ♠ Q J 10 6                      ♠ A 8 2
  ♡ 7 3          N                ♡ K 8 2
  ◇ Q 8 3    W       E            ◇ K J 7 6 4
  ♣ K Q 6 5      S                ♣ J 4
                    ♠ K 5
                    ♡ Q 10 5
                    ◇ 10 5 2
                    ♣ 10 9 8 3 2
```

YOU	LHO	PARTNER	RHO
Pass	1♡	Pass	2♡
?			

On the previous deal, you held the shortage in their suit in the reopening seat. Here, you sit directly over the raiser but the situation remains much the same.

Against opponents playing 4-card majors, who might have only a 4-3 fit, it is dangerous to compete or protect when holding three cards in their suit – if the suit splits 4-3-3-3 round the table, there could be no 8-card or better fit for anyone. In this case, you want to avoid finding yourself at the 3-level with only half the high cards. Still, you must play with the odds.

If Two Hearts is passed to your partner, he cannot easily tell whether to reopen. As you have the shortage in the enemy suit, the duty falls on you once more to take some positive action. Your initial pass limited your hand, making this a relatively safe takeout double. By making this call you find the cold 3◇.

There was a time when people would only make this sort of double in match-point pairs events. Nowadays, experienced players appreciate the value of a part-score and a plus score at other forms of scoring. Playing rubber, 60 below the line on your side leaves you feeling much happier than 60 below on theirs. At teams scoring, transforming –110 into +110 (if they allow you to buy the contract) or +100 (if they bid on and go down) represents a 5-IMP swing.

	♠ A K 4		♠ 10 6 2
	♡ 6 3		♡ A Q 10
	◇ Q J 6 2		◇ K 10 7 4 3
	♣ K 10 7 4		♣ A 2

YOU	LHO	PARTNER	RHO
–	1NT	Pass	2◇ *
Pass	2♡	Pass	Pass
?			

Sometimes you can make game despite a weak no-trump opening from an opponent. However, despite possessing a combined 26 HCP, getting into the auction may prove problematic. This partly comes about because partner was unable to enter the auction safely – for all he knew, responder might have held your 13 HCP and been planning to rebid 3NT after the transfer to offer a choice of games.

It was only when RHO passed opener's completion of the transfer that his weakness became clear. Fortunately, you hold the shortage in hearts, which gives you a straightforward re-opening double. This enables partner to call the laydown 3NT. *Competing when short in their suit can protect partner*.

	♠ 4		♠ K 10 9 8 2
	♡ A J 7 6 3		♡ Q 4
	◇ K Q 10 4		◇ A 7 2
	♣ A 8 2		♣ 7 4 3

YOU	LHO	PARTNER	RHO
1♡	2♠	Pass	Pass
?			

Your LHO has clearly chosen the wrong time to come in with a jump overcall. Can you find a way to punish him?

If, as most tournament players do these days, you use negative doubles, partner lacks the option to double for business. Thankfully, all is not lost as you are still there with a shortage in the overcaller's suit. When you reopen with a takeout double, partner will happily convert to penalties by passing. *Competing when short in their suit can collect a penalty if partner has been unable to double*.

	YOU	LHO	PARTNER	RHO
♠ 4				
♡ A 10 7 3	–	–	–	1♠
◊ J 9 6 4	?			
♣ Q 8 6 2				

Whilst you have both shortage in the suit opened and good support for all unbid suits, the hand is simply too weak for a takeout double. Remember that a takeout double on the first round suggests something like a minimum opening bid (or better). With a reasonable fit for one of your suits, partner will too often carry you overboard. He might instead jump to 2NT or leave One Spade Doubled in, which could prove equally disastrous.

If you pass, you may still get another chance. Suppose LHO raises to Two Spades, which comes back to you. Then, you can reassess the situation and back in with a double.

	YOU	LHO	PARTNER	RHO
♠ 6				
♡ Q 10 6 4	–	1♠	Pass	Pass
◊ J 8 7 3	?			
♣ Q 9 5 3				

Again, you hold the perfect shape for a double. Moreover, you can take a much more aggressive stance in fourth seat. Even so, limits do exist – a useful rule of thumb is to mentally add a king to your hand and then bid as you would have done if the opening bid had been on your right. Adding an extra 3 HCP to this hand would still leave it well short of the requirements for a takeout double of a One Spade opening. *Do not compete when short in their suit if your hand is too weak*.

Time and again, we hear players use the fact that their partner might have a 'penalty double' or 'trap pass' hand as an excuse to stretch a reopening double. There are several points to keep in mind here. Firstly, if your hand is bad, the opposing contract may succeed even if partner holds good values and length in their suit. Secondly, he stands more of a chance of having a balanced hand with four cards in their suit; this tends to limit him to at best a poor 15-count. Thirdly, if your hand contains less than its fair share of values, you can expect the overall HCPs to split either 23-17 or 22-18 to the opposition's advantage.

♠ 6	YOU	LHO	PARTNER	RHO
♡ Q 10 8 6	–	1♣	Pass	Pass
◇ K J 8 7 4 2	?			
♣ K 6				

We consider this a tough call, particularly at match-points. Clearly, partner holds some values. Why, in that case, has he elected not to come in over One Club? Most likely, he holds a balanced hand, including reasonable club length.

The other key question is 'Where do the spades lie?' Surely, partner would overcall if he held five of them. It seems, therefore, that the opponents have at least eight spades and perhaps more.

You can easily foresee what might happen if you reopen with One Diamond . . . The auction may continue 1♠-Pass-2♠. Still worse, you could hear 2♠-Pass-3♠ – and now you expect opener to raise to game. How happy would you feel then?

All in all, the right action is probably to let LHO toil away in his One Club contract. It sounds all too likely that reopening will allow the opponents to find a better strain.

♠ J 9 6 5	YOU	LHO	PARTNER	RHO
♡ Q 8 7 4	–	–	Pass	1◇
◇ 10 3	Pass	2◇	Pass	Pass
♣ A 10 3	?			

On this deal, your side appears to be outgunned. You only have a 7-count and partner could not open the bidding, so the opponents surely hold at least 22 points between them. If this is a match-point pairs sequence, you should feel glad that they have subsided in a minor. From the look of your hand, they may very well score better in no-trumps – you hold no 5-card suit to cause any damage and little reason to suppose partner does. If you enter the fray, you give them the chance to correct to 2NT and also the opportunity to double you. Cut your losses and pass. ***Do not compete when short in their suit if they appear to be in the wrong strain***.

For the last few examples, the opponents have given you the chance to bid at a low level. In real life, they often rule out this option! Let us now consider some higher-level decisions.

♠ Q 7 2	YOU	LHO	PARTNER	RHO
♡ J 4	–	–	1♠	4♣
◇ A J 9 4	?			
♣ 10 6 4 3				

Are you thinking of bidding Four Spades?

If so, then ask yourself how many spades you planned to bid if RHO had passed over One Spade. Surely, you would have made a simple raise to Two Spades and considered any other action a distinct overbid. You would have laughed if anyone had suggested you should raise to game, would you not?

If jumping to Four Spades in an uncontested auction seems crazy, it is surely wrong to be railroaded into bidding game by an opponent's pre-empt, which often heralds bad breaks.

Pass for now – if partner re-opens with a double, which would show significant extra values, you could consider removing to Four Spades at that point. In fact you might very well pass again, which is only likely to be wrong if partner has a void in clubs.

♠ Q 8 7 4	YOU	LHO	PARTNER	RHO
♡ 7 4	1♣	1♡	Double *	4♡
◇ A 9	?			
♣ A Q 9 6 3				

This situation resembles the previous one. Unless you have an unusual agreement about negative doubles in this situation, partner's double told you that your side has a 4-4 spade fit. So, are you going to bid Four Spades?

If RHO had passed, you intended to bid spades at what level: One Spade, perhaps Two Spades . . . Would you have dreamed of jumping to Four Spades with your 12 HCP facing the 6+ HCP promised by partner's double?

Surely only the world's greatest optimist would do so, and neither should you contemplate bidding game now. Once again, if partner reopens with an 'extra value showing' double of Four Hearts, you will have to decide whether to defend or declare. ***Do not compete when short in their suit if you would have to go two levels above your normal one***.

	YOU	LHO	PARTNER	RHO
♠ K Q 6 4 2			1NT	Pass
♡ J 7	–	–		
◇ 7 4	2♡ *	Pass	2♠	Pass
♣ K 9 8 6	Pass	3◇	Pass	Pass
	?			

Throughout this book you will hear us referring to the law of total tricks, so a brief explanation might help. The concept is very simple. The total number of tricks the two sides can take, each with their choice as trumps, equates to the combined length of their respective fits. So, if you have 8 spades and can make 2♠, then if they have 8 diamonds, they should be able to make 2◇. Alternatively, if you can make nine tricks, they can take only seven and so on. On this hand, your side possesses at best an 8-card spade fit (partner has had two chances to bid 3♠ with four) and the opponents hold at most nine diamonds (partner's 1NT promises two). This gives a maximum of 17 total trumps, which suggests one side's 3-level contract will make and the other's will fail. More likely, there are only 16 total trumps, in which case bidding 3♠ could turn a plus into a minus. If you had to bid, we would prefer a double, but this strikes us as rather risky on an aceless hand opposite a 12-14 1NT. *Do not compete when short in their suit if doing so violates the law of total tricks*.

	YOU	LHO	PARTNER	RHO
♠ K 5				
♡ K 10 6 4 2	–	1♣	Pass	1♡
◇ A 9 7 4	Pass	2♣	Pass	Pass
♣ Q 3	?			

We can give two reasons to pass. Firstly, the opponents have not found a fit, which means you may not have one either. Indeed, the chances appear against it since RHO has called your longest suit.

You can work out the second from the question 'What could you bid?' One option is to try a natural Two Hearts, but that should show a much better suit than this. Remember that RHO must hold at least four hearts and will often turn up with five. The only other alternative is a takeout double, inviting partner to choose between the unbid suits. Do you really want him to choose his 4-card spade suit on this hand? You can see this coming. *Do not compete when short in their suit if you cannot stand partner's likely response*.

♠ 10 7 4	YOU	LHO	PARTNER	RHO
♡ J 3	–	1♠	Pass	2♡
◇ A J 6 5	?			
♣ A Q 7 4				

Yes, you have an opening bid and sound support for both unbid suits. For all that, where do you think you are heading on this deal?

The likelihood that you can make game without some wild shape is exceedingly slim when the opponents possess enough strength for an opening bid and a two-over-one response. The fact that they own the majors further reduces your chance of buying the contract at all.

The likely result of entering with a takeout double is to offer the opposition 'fielder's choice' – they can bid and make their game or they can double you for a large penalty. ***Do not compete when short in their suit if you figure to be outgunned***.

♠ 7 4	YOU	LHO	PARTNER	RHO
♡ A J 9 7 6 4	1♡	2◇	Pass	3♣
◇ 6	?			
♣ A K J 4				

Do you feel like bidding Three Hearts? The only excuse for doing so is that your bidding box came without any 'Pass' cards!

Two possible hand types exist for partner – a bad hand with poor heart support (i.e., with too little strength for a negative double and not enough hearts to raise) or a penalty double of Two Diamonds.

If he turns up with the weak hand, you are outgunned and the opponents may double Three Hearts. This represents bad news on two counts – not only will you go for a sizeable penalty but, if you pass Three Clubs, the opponents may well bid a game and go down.

Things work out no better if partner holds the stronger hand type. If he planned to double them at the 2-level, the penalty will be even larger a level higher, and they scarcely seem to have found a better spot. Indeed, if Three Clubs is passed back to him, he can double to show a penalty double of diamonds, and you will gladly pass.

Alas, if you bid Three Hearts, you will miss a juicy penalty. Worse still, partner will bid again, 3NT most likely, and you will probably end up minus. ***Do not compete when short in their suit if bidding could stop partner from penalizing the opponents***.

♠ 7	YOU	LHO	PARTNER	RHO
♡ Q 8 6 5	–	–	Pass	1♠
◇ A 10 7 4 3	Pass	2♠	Pass	Pass
♣ J 6 5	?			

You are short in the enemy suit with support for all three unbid suits and the opponents have ground to a halt at the 2-level. This means you reopen with a double, right?

Just ask yourself one quick question – how many points do the opponents have? It would seem that they have at least 23-24 because you can see only seven and partner failed to open the bidding. What might reopening therefore achieve?

Yes, you might push the opponents to the 3-level. You might also reopen and hear the auction continue 3♠-Pass-4♠. These things happen! You might then concede 620 instead of the –170 you could have scored by passing out Two Spades. *Do not compete when short in their suit if the enemy seems to have missed game*.

Golden Rule Two:

Competing When Short in Their Suit can

. . . Help you find your own best contract;
. . . Push your opponents up a level;
. . . Protect partner;
. . . Collect a penalty when partner has been unable to double.

Do not Compete When Short in Their Suit if

. . . Your hand is too weak;
. . . They appear to be in the wrong strain;
. . . You would have to go two levels above your normal one;
. . . Doing so violates the law of total tricks;
. . . You cannot stand partner's likely response;
. . . You figure to be outgunned;
. . . Bidding could stop partner from penalizing the opponents;
. . . The enemy seems to have missed game.

Rule Three: Compete via a Double

You will frequently find yourself wanting to bid, either to enter or to stay in the auction, but without a sensible way to describe your hand. A double (normally for take-out) will often prove an effective solution.

One obvious advantage of such a double lies in its flexibility: it serves both to show values and consult your partner whilst leaving all options open, including defending. If you study the monthly bidding panel competition in any bridge magazine, you will observe that the expert commentators solve many a problem via a double. If it works for them, it can for you.

	YOU	LHO	PARTNER	RHO
♠ A Q 9 4	–	–	–	1♡
♡ 6	Double	3♡	Pass	Pass
◇ K Q 10 7	?			
♣ A K J 6				

Are you going to pass and allow LHO to buy the contract with his pre-emptive raise? Partner might have passed because he has only a few scattered values – remember you only promised a minimum opening bid with your takeout double of One Heart. You can well imagine having game available your way, particularly if partner has spade length, and making at least a part-score seems odds on. Still, do you really want to guess which of your 4-card suits will best fit partner's hand?

The answer, as you have probably worked out already, is to double again. This simply says to partner, 'I still have a takeout double of hearts but I can offer significant extra values.' Partner will usually hold support for one of your three suits. He will remove to his longest suit at a minimum level with a weak hand. If he possesses some real values, he can safely jump to game once he knows about your extras.

Naturally, partner may want to defend Three Hearts Doubled. He was unable to make a penalty double at his first turn: a double of Three Hearts by partner would have been 'Responsive' – asking you to pick a suit. You give him the option of passing again, and thus converting your second double for penalties.

♠ K Q 5	YOU	LHO	PARTNER	RHO
♡ 9	–	–	–	1♡
◇ A Q 10 7 6 5	2◇	2♡	Pass	Pass
♣ A 9 6	?			

Whilst your 2-level overcall suggested a decent 6-card suit, you would surely bid the same way without the ♣A or one of the spade pictures. This means you should make another effort – either to buy the contract for your side or to push the other side a level higher.

You can rule out Three Diamonds; it would imply a 7-card suit. You cannot call one of the black suits on only three cards either, yet you would happily accept one of them as trumps if partner held five.

Again, an 'extra values' double fits the bill. This is for takeout, and suggests tolerance for both unbid suits, but you could have a 3-2-6-2 shape. The main message is more high cards than your earlier bid showed. *Competing via a double can announce extra values.*

Partner might leave in your double on one of the examples above, but this hardly ever happens at such low levels. When the auction is already at game (or above), pass becomes a live possibility . . .

♠ K 5 2	YOU	LHO	PARTNER	RHO
♡ 6 4	–	1♡	Double	4♡
◇ Q 10 8 2	?			
♣ A J 9 4				

You have enough to believe your side owns the deal, but what is the best spot? If partner can produce a decent 5-card suit, you might make game in his suit. What if he holds a classic 4-1-4-4 shape?

You might guess to bid one of your suits at the 5-level, but doing so could easily prove disastrous. Bidding 4NT to invite partner to choose a minor rates to work more often, but could also backfire.

If you have enough high cards to score 11 tricks on an 8-card fit, you can expect to extract a useful penalty from Four Hearts Doubled. More to the point, when you can make only ten tricks in your minor, you still rate to defeat Four Hearts Doubled by a trick or two.

Doubling Four Hearts provides the answer. This is not a penalty double – partner knows this as RHO frequently holds five hearts for his jump to the 4-level. This optional double merely says, 'I have some values but no long suit to bid. Do you want to play or defend?'

♠ K 6	YOU	LHO	PARTNER	RHO
♡ Q 10 7 6 4	–	–	1♣	4♠
◇ J 4 2	?			
♣ A 10 3				

Once more, your hand contains more values than partner might expect, but do you really want to commit to a 5-level contract?

Sure, you might manage to make eleven (or more) tricks in either hearts or clubs. Then again, you may have no fit: your partner could be 3-2-4-4 (unless you play that you always open 1◇ with that).

As we discussed on the previous deal, even finding an 8-card fit at the 5-level rarely produces the best result. For example, put partner with a 3-1-4-5 or 3-2-3-5 shape; do you really think that trying to take four tricks will prove harder than going for eleven, particularly when your suits all rate to break badly?

In this situation, again, double simply shows values. If he holds a wildly distributional collection, partner will remove your double and he should like your dummy. With a balanced hand, he will leave it in and you should collect a nice penalty. *Competing via a double can avoid committing to a high-level contract*.

♠ K 8	YOU	LHO	PARTNER	RHO
♡ A 10 7 5 3 2	1♡	2◇	2♠	3◇
◇ 7 4	?			
♣ A Q 8				

The opponents have found a fit, so you do not want to defend. But do you want to play this hand in hearts, spades, or possibly clubs?

You know little about partner's hand. Is he 5-2-2-4, when you have an 8-card heart fit? Perhaps he holds a 6-1-2-4 shape (when spades is probably your best suit) or maybe a 5-1-2-5, when you might want to get into a club contract.

A double here asks for takeout since the opponents have found a fit at a low level. It primarily conveys the message, 'I definitely want to bid but do not know what.' Partner will appreciate that you have something like fairly good hearts, a partial spade fit and maybe a secondary club suit. Armed with that much knowledge about your assets, partner will do the right thing most of the time. *Competing via a double can preserve flexibility about strain*.

♠ A J 10 9 6 4	YOU	LHO	PARTNER	RHO
♡ A K Q	–	–	–	1 any
♢ A 6	?			
♣ K 4				

We generally advocate making an overcall to show your long suit at your first turn intending to double later to convey your extra values. Still, you can take a good principle too far, and this hand looks far too strong to start with a simple One Spade bid. A good rule of thumb is that if you are too strong to go 1NT, you are too good to overcall in a suit. Otherwise, you are gambling that the auction keeps going.

Here you must start with a takeout double. You will then bid your spades at an appropriate level at your second turn. Note that you need quite a strong hand to adopt this approach because you might find the auction at the 4-level when you get a second go. On this collection, you might happily bid Four Spades should the need arise. *Competing via a double can save you from limiting your hand*.

♠ Q 9 6 5	YOU	LHO	PARTNER	RHO
♡ K 4	–	–	–	2♢ *
♢ A 10 6	?			
♣ A 9 4 2				

Conventional bids such as the Multi Two Diamonds can prove very effective, but they also suffer from a drawback that you should aim to exploit when your opponents use such weapons against you.

Defending against the Multi, you get two chances to enter the auction. A delayed double, once you know opener's suit, best serves the function of a normal takeout double.

What do you think about an immediate double of the opening bid? Remember that LHO is still in the dark regarding his partner's hand, which makes it relatively risk-free for you to enter the auction. You should, therefore, take this opportunity to describe this type of hand, one that would be silenced by a natural weak two opening bid – a balanced hand with minimum opening bid values.

If partner holds something similar, you might manage to reach a good game on a deal where a natural weak two or a weak no-trump opening by RHO would mean that you pass throughout. *Competing via a double can show values safely*.

♠ A Q 9 7 6 5	YOU	LHO	PARTNER	RHO
♡ A 8 7	1♠	2♣	Pass	Pass
◇ K J 4	?			
♣ 2				

We saw earlier how a double at the game level offered your side the option of defending, rather than advancing beyond your depth.

Sometimes, a low-level double also allows you to defend. In the auction shown above, it seems quite possible that partner would want to make a penalty double of Two Clubs: you have a singleton club yet RHO failed to raise. Of course, your partner could not double LHO's overcall because doing so would have been a negative double. To catch your opponents when they enter the auction unwisely you must find another way.

After a simple overcall, virtually any opening bid with a shortage in the overcaller's suit should re-open. Most often, as here, you will do so with a double. *Competing via a double can allow for the fact that partner may want to defend.*

♠ J 9 6	YOU	LHO	PARTNER	RHO
♡ K 7	–	1♣	1♡	1♠
◇ A Q 10 6 5	?			
♣ 10 7 3				

Should you introduce your diamonds? If so, do you reckon partner will rebid a moderate 6-card heart suit? Maybe you should support his hearts despite holding only a doubleton? Of course, to do so could look rather silly if partner turns up with 5-4 in the red suits. Perhaps some alternative action would keep both options open . . .

A competitive double usually indicates length in both unbid suits. This auction illustrates the exception – there is only one unclaimed suit. A double in this situation remains conventional: it shows length in the single unbid suit and a partial fit for partner's suit. *Competing via a double can say you have two places to play.*

On this example, it was clear that you meant the double for takeout because RHO's bid was forcing. If you really had a spade stack, you would wait for them to get higher. If the opponents agree a suit, it should appear equally obvious that you do not want to double for penalties at a low level.

♠ Q J 6 5		♠ Q J 6 5
♡ K 10 7 4	or	♡ K 7
◇ 6		◇ A J 6 2
♣ J 8 5 2		♣ Q 10 5

YOU	LHO	PARTNER	RHO
–	1◇	Double	2◇
?			

Holding the first of the two hands above, you want to compete, but which of your 4-card suits should you choose?

A responsive double means you can avoid deciding. This type of double says to partner, 'I hold some values and support for at least two unbid suits, you pick.' When you have only moderate values, as with this first hand, it will always contain support for unbid majors.

The second hand presents a similar problem. You want to bid game, but should it be in spades or in no-trumps? After all, partner will sometimes produce fewer than four spades for a takeout double.

Again, starting with a responsive double provides the answer. If you then discover that partner has four spades, you can go ahead and bid game in that strain. If instead he bids something like 2♡ at his second turn, and then 3♣ over your forcing 2♠ continuation, you can show your diamond stopper(s) by bidding 3NT. *Competing via a double can avoid stressing one feature*.

Most of the doubles we have seen so far have been for takeout. Your side collects a penalty when one of you holds values and the other, with length in their suit, elects to leave in the double. You may be relieved to hear that, even in the 21st century, some low-level doubles do retain a penalty meaning. Doubles made by a player who cannot sensibly want a takeout express a desire to penalize.

	YOU	LHO	PARTNER	RHO
♠ J 4	–	–	–	1♡
♡ K J 9 6	Pass	Pass	Double	2◇
◇ A 7 4	?			
♣ Q J 10 4				

Too weak with no shape to act directly over One Heart, you would probably have jumped to 2NT if RHO had passed at his second turn. His actual Two Diamonds opens up another possibility.

Partner's takeout double implies tolerance for the unbid suits (or a strong hand). Looking at it another way, he ought to have enough diamonds or overall strength to cope with a Two Diamond response from you. This makes A-x-x more than adequate to double. It is clearly for penalties as you could have doubled 1♡ for takeout or bid 2♡ now to ask partner for a suit. Note that you need to consider your heart holding for this sequence. There is little point doubling Two Diamonds if you know a 2♡ preference will leave you fixed.

♠ Q J 10 9 7 5	YOU	LHO	PARTNER	RHO
♡ A 8	–	–	–	1NT
◇ 6 3	?			
♣ A K 4				

Doubles of their 1NT opening convey a slightly different meaning. Whilst they still announce values, partner now has no duty to remove your double. Against a weak no-trump, most people play that you double on any hand stronger than the opener's. So, when 1NT shows 12-14, you need 15 plus. Against a strong no-trump, you can play it the same way, but more often you might double holding a good suit to lead. With this hand, you would certainly double a weak no-trump and you might do the same to a strong one – although passing smoothly and hoping that LHO raises to 3NT could work a treat! *Competing via a double can let you pick up a useful penalty*.

♠ K 9 4	YOU	LHO	PARTNER	RHO
♡ A K 8 6 5	1♡	2◇	2♡	3◇
◇ 5	?			
♣ A J 9 3				

If the auction given here were uncontested, you would have plenty of room to make a descriptive game try over partner's single raise. Alas, this opposing bidding leaves you with no room at all. Clearly, you need the option to bid Three Hearts as a purely competitive move, without fear that partner will take you seriously and raise. How, then, can you try for game?

The solution is to use a double for this purpose. Remember, you do not make low-level penalty doubles when the opponents find a fit. *Competing via a double can enable you to make a game try*.

♠ 9 6 5	YOU	LHO	PARTNER	RHO
♡ K 7 4	1♢	Pass	1♡	2♣
♢ A Q 10 6 3	?			
♣ K 7				

The 'Support Double', a convention that was invented by Jeff Meckstroth and Eric Rodwell, has gained widespread popularity both throughout the USA and elsewhere. It applies in auctions such as the one illustrated above – you open, partner responds (usually in a major), and RHO overcalls at the minimum level.

You will want to make a minimum heart raise on all kinds of hands including both 3-card and 4-card support. Since LHO will frequently raise his partner's overcall, it will often prove vital for your partner to find out exactly how good your trump fit is – the more trumps you have between you, the better your offensive prospects and the worse they are defending. Using a (support) double to show any hand with 3-card support provides the answer. You can make a descriptive bid or double again later to convey extra values with a hand stronger than a limit raise. This means that an immediate raise of partner's suit promises 4-card support. *Competing via a double can show three-card support.*

♠ K 6	YOU	LHO	PARTNER	RHO
♡ J 8 7 4 2	–	1♡	1♠	2♣
♢ 5	Pass	2♡	Pass	2♠
♣ J 9 7 6 5	?			

You could hardly support partner's spades with only a doubleton, but you certainly want him to lead the suit if LHO should become declarer, particularly in a no-trump contract. RHO's cue bid, which presumably asks his partner to bid no-trumps with a spade stopper, gives you the opportunity for a lead-directing double. (This closely resembles a Rosenkranz double, named after George Rosenkranz). *Competing via a double can ask for the suit to be led.*

As an aside, the more system-minded amongst you might be interested to learn that many top-level partnerships reverse the meaning of pass and double in this type of auction. The logic behind this derives from the fact that LHO will often be stuck for a sensible bid when he has nothing in your side's suit.

This will most often happen when you hold a high card in the suit, but a double from you provides him with the option of passing. By contrast, if you pass to express a liking for spades, LHO has to find a bid. Equally, when you hold nothing in partner's suit, LHO may well bid no-trumps no matter what you do, so a double costs nothing.

	YOU	LHO	PARTNER	RHO
♠ A Q 8 6 5				
♡ A 4	1♠	2♠ *	Pass	3♣ *
♢ 4	?			
♣ K J 7 6 4				

LHO's Michael's cue bid shows hearts and a minor. RHO's Three Clubs asks him to pass (with clubs) or to convert to Three Diamonds. At first sight, it seems unclear whether double from you is takeout of clubs or says you hold clubs. Actually, you can have the best of both worlds! If LHO passes, your double asks for takeout. If he retreats to 3♢ (as will no doubt happen here), double shows clubs.

You can use the two-way double in any auction where RHO makes a 'pass or correct' bid. The other obvious example is a 2♢ Multi on your left and a 2♡ relay response on your right (to play opposite a weak two in hearts). In this case, your double can show a takeout of hearts if LHO passes and hearts if he does anything else. *Competing via a double can be a two-way move*.

	YOU	LHO	PARTNER	RHO
♠ J 8 7 6 5				
♡ –	1♠	2♡	Pass	Pass
♢ A K Q 10 2	?			
♣ K J 2				

Several times now, you have re-opened (or competed) with a double half expecting partner to convert this into a penalty double.

Still, occasions crop up when you would have pulled a penalty double from partner. Defending at low levels with a void in trumps rarely brings joy. Indeed, it appears particularly unattractive on this collection since partner may well lead from something like king and another spade in response to your opening bid.

For sure, you must find a rebid on this shape, but doubling just asks for trouble. We recommend Three Diamonds. *Do not compete via a double when you cannot stand a penalty pass*.

♠ 5	YOU	LHO	PARTNER	RHO
♡ K 10 7 4	–	–	–	1♣
◇ A Q J 9 6	?			
♣ K J 4				

Yes, you have sound opening bid values, but you also need the right shape for a takeout double. That means adequate support for all of the unbid suits.

If you make a takeout double of RHO's One Club on this hand, in which suit do you think partner will respond? What is more, he might keep on bidding those spades of his with something like ♠Q-x-x-x-x. He would be quite within his rights to do so, since you promised at least 3-card support (or significant extra values). His face will drop when you put down dummy with a singleton trump in Three or Four Spades (probably doubled). You must hope he forgives easily.

♠ 7	YOU	LHO	PARTNER	RHO
♡ J 4	1♣	2♠	Pass	Pass
◇ A J 10 7	?			
♣ A K J 8 6 5				

Yes, your hand contains a singleton in LHO's suit and you have a decent opening bid, so you can scarcely pass. True, partner may wish to defend Two Spades Doubled. Even so, it would be wrong to re-open with a double.

The reason is that partner may not have a penalty double of spades. He may just hold a poor hand with, say, a 4-5-2-2 or 4-4-4-1 shape or something similar. If so, to which suit do you think he will remove your double? Right – he will go for the unbid major.

You lack the strength to advance to the 4-level opposite a bad hand with probable shortage in your long suit. Equally, J-x constitutes inadequate support to leave partner playing in that suit at the 3-level.

As those are the only two options if you double and partner removes to Three Hearts, you cannot re-open with a double of Two Spades. You must either rebid your 6-card club suit or bid 2NT (if your partner would understand this as Unusual, implying good clubs and a diamond suit). *Do not compete via a double when partner's take-out action may embarrass you*.

♠ A J 9 6 5	YOU	LHO	PARTNER	RHO
♡ Q 10 7	–	–	1♣	1♠
◇ 8 6 3	?			
♣ A 2				

You cannot have your cake and eat it. When playing negative doubles, no matter how hard you slam the double card on the table (or how loudly you say double) it does not mean penalties. Partner can and will take it out. He will expect you to produce support for the unbid suits, particularly hearts.

Fortunately, as we saw earlier in this chapter, all is not lost. If you want to defend One Spade Doubled, you must pass (without hesitating and making it obvious to everyone that you hold a penalty double of spades). Much of the time, partner will re-open with a double and you can convert for penalties.

♠ Q 4	YOU	LHO	PARTNER	RHO
♡ K 8 4	–	–	–	3◇
◇ A Q J 7	?			
♣ A K 10 6				

Most good players these days play double for take-out over a three bid (in both the direct and protective positions). If you have agreed that a double requests a takeout, doubling on this hand and hoping partner will work out that you intend it for penalties this time is asking the impossible. He never will!

If you double, your partner will probably jump to Four Spades on his J-x-x-x-x, expecting you to have at least 3-card support for an unbid major. As a result, you will land in a silly contract with Three No-trumps (clearly the proper bid on a hand like this) an easy make. *Do not compete via a double when its meaning does not match your system*.

On both these hands it was crystal clear what a double from you would mean. As we alluded to earlier, you may get the impression reading panel articles that experts double to get themselves out of any difficulty and say that a double describes perfectly the particular hand in front of them! We can assure you that real life works a bit differently. A good partnership would have agreements (or at least principles) about what doubles mean.

♠ A 6 4	YOU	LHO	PARTNER	RHO
♡ K 10 6 5	–	–	–	1♠
◇ Q 7	Pass	Pass	2◇	2♠
♣ J 10 8 4	?			

Given that a double from you would have been for take-out on the previous round, it would be normal to regard this as a penalty situation. Note that this situation falls outside the general principle discussed earlier. Yes, the opponents are at a low level but they have not found a fit – RHO has bid spades twice without any support from his partner.

Unless you and your partner have specifically agreed to play a double for takeout in this sequence, you must not 'double and hope he works it out'. It is in this way that you quickly learn all about scores such as –670, –730, etc. Knowing that partner can bid again if he wishes to look for game somewhere, you should just raise to 3◇. *Do not compete via a double when a misunderstanding beckons.*

♠ 3	YOU	LHO	PARTNER	RHO
♡ K 10 7 6 5	–	1♠	Pass	2♣
◇ K J 8 6 4 3	?			
♣ 4				

Yes, a double would be for takeout, implying the two unbid suits, but partner will expect a different type of hand. A double indicates more in terms of high cards and defensive values, perhaps with only 4-4 or 5-4 in the red suits. It implies convertible values with which you would feel happy for partner to double the opponents if he thinks they have overstretched. This hand falls well short on that reckoning.

Nobody says that you have to pass on this moderate hand. Your playing strength appears potentially excellent if partner fits one or both of your suits. Quite possibly, both sides can make a fairly large number of tricks with their best suit as trumps. If you want to bid on this two-suiter, you should come in with an Unusual Two No-trumps – promising length in both unbid suits and only moderate (at best) defensive values. It is then up to partner to decide whether to bid a game or, perhaps, to sacrifice at a high level in one of your suits. He might yet double the opponents, but you can rest assured he will not be relying on you to take defensive tricks if he does.

♠ 6 5 4	YOU	LHO	PARTNER	RHO
♡ 6	Pass	Pass	Pass	1♡
◇ A Q 10 6	?			
♣ K J 9 7 5				

Holding at least three cards in each unbid suit, the player who held these cards at the table elected to double. It seemed like a good idea at the time, but when the auction continued 4♡, 4♠, Double the risk became apparent. Partners tend to assume that when there is only one unbid major, you will have 4-card support for it, especially when they know you cannot hold reserves of values. This makes doubling highly dangerous.

As we just saw, you need a lot of shape for an unusual 2NT bid. Here, having passed as dealer, you can safely use 1NT for the minors and a 5-4 shape will suffice. Who knows, if LHO raises to Two Hearts, you might reopen with a double to show your spade fragment and complete a more or less perfect description. *Do not compete via a double when a two-suited bid describes your hand better*.

♠ 4	YOU	LHO	PARTNER	RHO
♡ 8 6 5 2	Pass	1♠	Pass	2♣
◇ A K J 10 7	?			
♣ Q 8 2				

Neither you nor your partner could muster a bid on the first round (although opening with a weak two in diamonds if you had one available would suit some tastes). Your hand contains adequate support for both unbid suits, so should you try a takeout double?

No – whilst you were both passing, the opponents have made an opening bid and a two-over-one response, leaving little likelihood that the deal belongs to your side. You are hardly ever going to outbid them after this start to the auction. What is important is that partner gets off to the best opening lead if LHO becomes declarer (in spades or no-trumps). If you want to bid, Two Diamonds stands out as the right action. Even a pass rates more highly than a double, since a double tends to focus partner's attention on the unbid major, which is exactly what you want to avoid. *Do not compete via a double when doing so may attract the wrong lead*.

♠ A J 10	YOU	LHO	PARTNER	RHO
♡ K J 10 7 5	–	–	–	1♢
♢ 6	?			
♣ A Q 6 3				

Bidding trends change over time and thirty years ago the accepted wisdom was to double on hands like this one. Nowadays most tournament-level partnerships have agreed to treat them by starting with an overcall, intending to double later to express their extra values if the auction allows.

There are numerous reasons why this method is superior. Most vitally, you run the risk of losing your 5-card major if you start with a double. Partner will not respond in a 3-card suit, and both your HCP and your suit fall short of the requirements to double and then bid Two Hearts over a minimum response in a black suit.

Suppose LHO jumps to Three Diamonds over your takeout double. If partner passes, do you intend to advance to Three Hearts all on your own? Surely you will pass, but this figures to backfire any time partner holds 4-card heart support. If you start with an overcall, partner will rarely sell out when he holds primary support. *Do not compete via a double when your long suit might become lost*.

♠ A Q	YOU	LHO	PARTNER	RHO
♡ K 9 4	–	–	–	1♠
♢ K J 7 3	?			
♣ K 10 6 5				

When the opposition open your shortest suit and you hold at least an opening bid, you will usually want to make a takeout double. This hand illustrates an exception.

Suppose you double. What will you do if partner responds Two Hearts? You could raise, but partner might easily hold only a 4-card suit. Perhaps you want to bid Two No-trumps. Sadly, that is no good either – it indicates a hand too good for an immediate One No-trump overcall (i.e., about 18/19-20/21 HCP).

Here you have a balanced 15-18 with at least one spade stopper. Surely a One No-trump overcall shows that? *Do not compete via a double when you have a more descriptive alternative*.

♠ K 6	YOU	LHO	PARTNER	RHO
♡ A Q 6 4 2	1♡	1♠	Double	3♠
◇ A 10 6	?			
♣ K J 7				

If you use a strong no-trump and feel comfortable about opening 1NT with a five-card major (playing 5-card Stayman perhaps), you would not find yourself in this position.

Partner's double is negative, suggesting at least moderate values and support for both unbid suits. Perhaps, therefore, you should make a responsive double. After all, a minor-suit game may be playable or partner might turn up with three hearts, allowing you to play game in that suit.

Now imagine he holds a dull 2-2-5-4 shape with plenty of points but no spade stopper. Do you expect him to bid 3NT with two low spades? He can hardly do that; he will bid his 5-card minor and you will end up in an awkward 11-trick game when Three No-trumps (your correct bid) may have nine top tricks.

♠ K 7 6	YOU	LHO	PARTNER	RHO
♡ A J 9 4	–	–	–	3♠
◇ A 8 6	?			
♣ A Q 5				

Yes, partner might have four hearts, in which case game in those may be easy. No doubt you will get there if you start with a double.

Unfortunately, a fair proportion of the time, he will hold fewer than four hearts and he will respond Four Clubs or Four Diamonds. Do you plan to retreat to 4NT? You will look a little foolish when that proves to be one level too high, will you not? Worse – perhaps partner will take 4NT as some form of Blackwood and tell you how many aces he holds.

Once again, a takeout double rates to lead the auction up to an uncomfortably high level. *Do not compete via a double when a sensible no-trump call keeps the bidding lower*.

We hope you have seen through this chapter how useful and flexible a double can be. Next time you feel like pulling a big pile of cards out of your bidding box, first consider whether a little red one will do the job!

Golden Rule Three:

Competing via a Double can

. . . Announce extra values;
. . . Avoid committing to a high-level contract;
. . . Preserve flexibility about strain;
. . . Save you from limiting your hand;
. . . Show values safely;
. . . Allow for the fact that partner may want to defend;
. . . Say you have two places to play;
. . . Avoid stressing one feature;
. . . Let you pick up a useful penalty;
. . . Enable you to make a game try;
. . . Show three-card support;
. . . Ask for the suit to be led;
. . . Be a two-way move.

Do not Compete via a Double when

. . . You cannot stand a penalty pass;
. . . Partner's take-out action may embarrass you;
. . . Its meaning does not match your system;
. . . A misunderstanding beckons;
. . . A two-suited bid describes your hand better;
. . . Doing so may attract the wrong lead;
. . . Your long suit might become lost;
. . . You have a more descriptive alternative;
. . . A sensible no-trump call keeps the bidding lower.

Rule Four: Cue-Bid the Enemy Suit

The cue bid was to the 1980s what the double has become in latter years – something of a panacea for numerous sorts of bidding problems. It still serves as a useful weapon, as we shall see.

	YOU	LHO	PARTNER	RHO
♠ Q 5				1♠
♡ A Q 7 5	–	–	–	
◇ A K 8	Double	Pass	2◇	Pass
♣ A Q J 4	2♠			

Can you think of another sensible action apart from 2♠?

Sure, 3NT might work, but so too might Five Diamonds or pass. A Two Spade cue bid merely says to partner: 'I have a very good hand with no limit bid available, please tell me more.' You will often hold exactly three cards in his suit, but you may have more or less.

Partner's Two Diamond response covers a fairly wide range. He could turn up with as little as this:

♠ 8 7 6 2
♡ 8 4
◇ 9 7 5 4
♣ 9 7 2

In this case, even making Three Diamonds will prove a struggle. He might also produce a hand suitable for 3NT:

♠ J 7 6 2
♡ 9 8 4
◇ Q J 5 4 2
♣ K

On another day, a slam might be on. Or, you may yet need to find your best strain – either clubs or hearts might play facing a 5-4 or 6-4 shape. At this stage, you could only hazard a guess about the final contract. So you should force partner to reveal more about his hand while, at the same time, telling him that you hold extra strength: bid 2♠. *Cue-bidding the enemy suit can announce general values*.

♠ K 6	YOU	LHO	PARTNER	RHO
♡ A 10 8 7 6 4	1♡	2♣	2♠	Pass
◇ K 8 3	?			
♣ A 2				

Do you want to play this deal in hearts, spades, no-trumps or even diamonds?

We could easily construct hands consistent with partner's initial response on which each of those four strains would prove the correct answer to the question. Therefore, at this point, you want to avoid committing your side to a final contract. You do, however, want to tell partner that you hold a suitable collection, and the way to do this is via a cue bid. *Cue-bidding the enemy suit can allow you to explore several spots*.

♠ A 6 5	YOU	LHO	PARTNER	RHO
♡ 6 2	–	1♡	1♠	Pass
◇ K 10 7 4 3	2♡			
♣ K 8 6				

Destructive bidding seems very much *de rigueur* in today's game. Thus, any raise of partner's overcall, whether a straightforward raise to the 2-level, a jump to Three Spades or an agricultural bash at game would all be understood as pre-emptive, or largely obstructive, in the vast majority of 21st Century partnerships.

Naturally, you will on occasion pick up a hand with support for partner and with genuine interest for him to take constructive action if he has a suitable overcall. Given that you can no longer show such features by raising spades, you must do so by calling the enemy's suit. Provided you sensibly play a change of suit response as forcing (so that game-going hands with no fit can go down that route), your Two Heart bid in the auction above promises at least a constructive raise to the 2-level. You might hold extra values, in which case you intend to make a further game try by bidding again if partner indicates a minimum by signing off. In some partnerships, a stronger hand will rarely contain four-card support because a jump cue bid shows such an animal. As only a limited number of people adopt this treatment, you would need to discuss this with your partner before wheeling out a jump cue bid to show a four-card raise at the table.

	YOU	LHO	PARTNER	RHO
♠ 9 6 3	YOU	LHO	1♡	2♣
♡ K 10 6 5	–	–		
◇ A Q J 6	3♣			
♣ J 4				

Jump raises in competitive sequences are generally played as pre-emptive by the opening side too – a jump to Three Hearts here would show a hand without, depending on the vulnerability, perhaps, the ♡K and/or ◇Q. Such bids can work as effective two-way shots: if partner holds some extra values he can probably come to nine tricks; if he has a minimum, the opponents might make something, often a game, and Three Hearts will prove a cheap sacrifice. Once again, you also need the ability to express a genuine, invitational raise such as the one here. One option is to employ a cue bid (Three Clubs in this auction) for such a purpose. *Cue-bidding the enemy suit can distinguish your hand from a pre-emptive raise.*

As an aside, you should note that if you do not play negative doubles (although you should), then you probably need to save this second type of cue bid for another meaning: a good hand on which you have nothing specific to say.

On the examples up until now, your cue bid has not promised a particular holding in the opponents' suit. It has merely conveyed a hand for which no other bid provides an adequate description. All this changes with our next few offerings.

	YOU	LHO	PARTNER	RHO
♠ A K 8	YOU	LHO	1♡	2♣
♡ Q 10 7 6 5	–	–		
◇ Q 7 4 3	4♣			
♣ 2				

You can virtually guarantee that you do not want to wind up in a high-level contract in a suit in which one opponent has announced significant length. RHO's overcall in the auction above suggests a good 5-card or, more often, a 6-card suit. This means you will never want to jump to Four Clubs in a natural sense.

Since this move also takes you past 3NT, it makes sense for it to indicate a positive fit for partner's suit. Using it to show both some interest beyond game and a shortage in the enemy suit will help you to reach some low point-count slams.

♠ K 9 4 2	YOU	LHO	PARTNER	RHO
♡ K 10 8 6	–	1◇	1♡	2◇
◇ –	4◇			
♣ A J 10 7 5				

The comments just made apply still more when your opponents agree a suit. For ease of memory, it makes sense to define a specific meaning for all jump cue bids. Using them as a splinter, to show support for partner and a shortage in the bid suit, is fairly universal. *Cue-bidding the enemy suit can indicate a shortage in it.*

♠ J 7 4	♠ Q 6
♡ A K 7	♡ Q 6 2
◇ K 6	◇ A Q 10 9 7 5
♣ Q 10 8 6 3	♣ K 2

YOU	LHO	PARTNER	RHO
–	–	1◇	1♠
2♣	Pass	2◇	Pass
?			

With these two hands, you want to end up in 3NT. How do you get there when neither of you has a full spade stopper? You must try 2♠ and partner can venture 3NT with his half stopper.

Now imagine partner keeps the same hand, and you hold this:

♠ A 5 3
♡ K 10 7
◇ J 4
♣ A J 8 6 5

This time you have a sure spade winner, but you still want to avoid calling no-trumps yourself. With the queen of spades protected, your side has two spade stoppers, which could make all the difference.

Please note that you may hear this sort of cue bid called either a directional asking bid, DAB for short or, in the US, a Western Cue Bid. The requirements for this can vary. Check with your partner what he sees as the minimum holding needed in their suit. *Cue-bidding the enemy suit can ask for a full or half stopper for 3NT.*

	YOU	LHO	PARTNER	RHO
♠ A J	YOU	LHO	PARTNER	RHO
♡ A J 10 8 7 6	–	–	1♣	1♠
◇ J 2	2♡	Pass	4♡	Pass
♣ Q 10 4	?			

Slam prospects appear excellent if you assume partner has some good clubs. Even so, you can hardly blast a slam or use Blackwood, as he could have two diamond losers:

♠ 10 2
♡ K Q 9 3
◇ Q 9
♣ A K J 8 7

The best way to avoid calling a slam off two fast losers in a side suit is to cue-bid controls. On this deal, you can indicate your slam interest and spade control with a Four Spade cue bid. Partner will, no doubt, bid Five Clubs to show his control there. When you retreat to Five Hearts, partner should infer you are concerned about diamonds.

With the hand given above, he will pass Five Hearts and you will score a safe game. If, however, he has a diamond control, he can go on. (If his control is the king, he should remember that you would declare a heart contract and perhaps try 6NT.) *Cue-bidding the enemy suit can denote a control in it for slam purposes.*

	YOU	LHO	PARTNER	RHO
♠ A Q J 7 6	YOU	LHO	PARTNER	RHO
♡ A K Q 10 4	–	–	–	1♣
◇ Q 8	?			
♣ 3				

Few people still use an immediate cue bid of the opener's suit in the traditional way to mean a powerhouse. Most tournament players nowadays use such cue bids to denote two-suited hands.

Numerous structures exist for expressing two-suited types after a major-suit opening, some of them truly weird and wonderful. By far the most popular is the Michaels Cue Bid, which shows a two-suited hand – both majors if they open a minor or, over a major, the unbid major and an undefined minor suit. You can have quite a weak hand, but here you plan to bid again. *Cue-bidding the enemy suit can show two suits at once.*

♠ K Q 8 6	YOU	LHO	PARTNER	RHO
♡ A 7 4 2	–	1♡	Double	Pass
◇ A J 5	?			
♣ 7 2				

If you were forced at gunpoint to guess the best contract right now, you would surely opt for Four Spades. After all, you are strong enough to expect to make game, and a take-out double of One Heart will contain a four-card spade suit more often than not.

However, no guarantees apply and it would be precipitous to commit yourself to game in spades when you have an alternative. There is no need to go leaping around with a strong hand. Simply tell your partner about your good values and create a forcing auction by cue-bidding the enemy suit. Having done that, you can use all the available space to investigate the best contract. *Cue-bidding the enemy suit can save you from having to jump to show strength*.

♠ 7 3	YOU	LHO	PARTNER	RHO
♡ Q 6 4 2	–	1◇	Double	1♠
◇ 10 4	?			
♣ A K 8 7 5				

This time, you could express your values accurately and show your best suit with a jump to Three Clubs. The problem is that it may turn out right to play the deal in hearts, rather than clubs.

A cue bid suggests more than one possible denomination and partner will work out that the choice on this deal lies between the rounded suits. As a takeout double tends to promise at least fair support for any unbid major, he will also figure out that your hearts are not your greatest asset. If they were – switch your hearts and clubs on the hand above, for example – you would simply introduce the major at the appropriate level and forget about your minor.

You should also note that you do not have a 'choice of cue bids' in this auction. Only Two Diamonds serves as a consultative action here. As we shall see in a moment, a spade bid from you would carry a different meaning altogether. *Cue-bidding the enemy suit can imply two places to play*.

♠ 7 4	YOU	LHO	PARTNER	RHO
♡ Q 7 5	1♣	1♡	1♠	Pass
◇ K J 5	1NT	Pass	3◇	Pass
♣ A K Q 9 6	?			

Your One No-trump rebid showed a stopper in the enemy's heart suit, but your holding appears distinctly less than robust. Queen to three usually works all right if you stop in One No-trump because if the opponents take the first five tricks it will not prove a disaster. Conversely, you would much rather avoid this situation when you have contracted for game in no-trumps. Moreover, partner's jump to Three Diamonds suggests some distribution, which increases the chance that he holds a heart shortage.

You would prefer not to raise diamonds with only 3-card support, and giving preference to spades on a low doubleton also seems far from ideal. Fortunately, a third possibility exists: a Three Heart cue bid expresses doubt about the final contract without overly stressing any particular feature. *Cue-bidding the enemy suit can express doubt about a stopper already shown*.

♠ A 4	YOU	LHO	PARTNER	RHO
♡ 4	–	–	–	1♡
◇ Q 6 2	?			
♣ A K Q J 9 7 5				

What do you suppose should become the final contract?

Perhaps some number of clubs will be right, but surely you would fancy your chances in Three No-trumps if partner can stop RHO's heart suit?

The problem is that no immediate club bid does justice to your playing strength, whilst starting with a takeout double may lead you to all manner of later problems. For example, if you ought to play in clubs, you will struggle to persuade partner of this when he holds only a singleton.

All you really want to say to partner is: 'I would like to play in Three No-trumps if you can stop hearts.' A jump cue bid of Three Hearts immediately over RHO's One Heart opening says exactly that. *Cue-bidding the enemy suit can announce a solid suit elsewhere (via a jump)*.

	YOU	LHO	PARTNER	RHO
♠ A Q 7	YOU	LHO	PARTNER	RHO
♡ 6 5	–	1♣	1◇	1♡
◇ Q 10 8 4	?			
♣ A 10 7 6				

When the opponents call two suits, you may have a choice of cue bids available. (This also applies when they imply two specific suits by using a convention such as a Michaels cue bid to show both majors.) Two workable methods cater for this situation . . .

One option is to use the lower cue bid like a negative double: length in the one unclaimed suit but too little to make a forcing bid. (You will usually also have tolerance for partner's suit.) The higher cue bid then denotes a value raise of partner's suit. The other method, especially useful when partner calls a minor, so making 3NT your most likely game, is to cue-bid the suit where you hold values.

Thus, using the second method, you would bid Two Clubs. This suggests game interest, a probable diamond fit, and something in clubs. You also implicitly deny heart values – with a stopper there, you could call no-trumps yourself. *Cue-bidding the enemy suit can indicate values in one of two enemy suits.*

	YOU	LHO	PARTNER	RHO
♠ K J 9 7 6 2	YOU	LHO	PARTNER	RHO
♡ 6 5	–	1♣	Double	1♠
◇ K 7 4	?			
♣ 7 3				

In the dim and distant past, a popular psyche was to bid a major suit you did not hold after an opponent's take-out double. One Spade in the auction above would frequently be made on a holding such as a low doubleton. If the bid were doubled, RHO would hastily retreat to opener's suit, for which he would invariably have support. This tactic remains in existence today, but you can combat it easily enough . . .

A double from you would not be negative, responsive or takeout. It would show positive values and spades, usually four but perhaps a poor 5-card suit. With a stronger holding, such as the one in the hand above, you need to bid spades yourself to get the message across.

Holding only these moderate values, Two Spades conveys the message. Give yourself another king in a red suit and you would jump to 3♠. *Cue-bidding the enemy suit can expose a psyche.*

You will need to remember this example whenever you hold both red suits and want partner to choose: neither a responsive double nor a 2♠ bid will create the desired effect. You would have to call 2♣.

So far we have encountered case after case on which following the rule, i.e., making a cue bid, solves the problem, albeit perhaps only for one round. As you would expect, this tactic cannot work on every deal. Sometimes you have a straightforward way to describe your hand. At others, what sounds like a cue bid to you may sound quite different to your partner. Consider this situation:

	YOU	LHO	PARTNER	RHO
♠ K 10 7 6				1♣
♡ J 8 6	–	–	–	
◇ Q 8 6	Pass	Pass	1◇	1NT
♣ K Q 3	?			

If you have specifically agreed to play a cue bid here (Two Clubs) as showing a constructive diamond raise, it describes this collection well. However, that would run contrary to the normal understanding of Two Clubs in this auction: logic suggests that on any strong hand you would start with a penalty double of opener's One No-trump.

Therefore, a bid of the enemy suit in an auction such as this would normally indicate an attempt to play there.

	YOU	LHO	PARTNER	RHO
♠ K 10 8 7 6 4				
♡ 6	–	1◇	Pass	1♡
◇ 4	?			
♣ A K 10 7 3				

In this situation, you must discount 2♡ as a possible cue bid. Bidding the suit called on your right is definitely natural. Opinions vary as to what 2◇ would mean. Particularly if the opening bid might be on a three-card suit, some people play this as natural. To go 2◇ with no agreement would court disaster. Sure, you would like to describe a two-suited hand with longer spades whilst keeping the auction at the 2-level, but only if you have agreed with your partner that a 2◇ cue bid carries this message should you try it out. Otherwise you should content yourself with an Unusual 2NT, which still shows the black suits and kills more of their bidding space. ***Do not cue-bid the enemy suit when partner may incorrectly interpret it as natural***.

♠ A 7 2	YOU	LHO	PARTNER	RHO
♡ K Q J 10 7 3	1♡	2♣	2♢	Pass
♢ Q 8	3♡			
♣ A 6				

A cue bid below game usually suggests that you cannot, for one reason or another, make a more descriptive bid. It may tell partner little about your hand other than that you possess sufficient values to create a force. Unfortunately, partner may find it equally difficult to make a decision, one that you could be now thrusting upon him.

It therefore stands to reason that you should only employ a cue bid when you lack a sensible alternative. The hand presented here offers you a perfectly reasonable descriptive bid: Three Hearts. This conveys both your extra values and your decent six-card heart suit. **Do not cue-bid the enemy suit when you have a clear alternative.**

♠ 7 6 3	YOU	LHO	PARTNER	RHO
♡ A J	–	–	1♢	1♠
♢ K 8 7	2♣	Pass	2♢	Pass
♣ K 10 7 4 2	3♢			

This time, you have a relatively balanced hand with the values for Two No-trumps. However, you can hardly bid no-trumps yourself with three low cards in RHO's spade suit. Switch your red-suit holdings, and you would be forced to cue-bid (Two Spades) – essentially asking partner if he holds a spade stopper.

Alas, all too often, your enquiry will simply allow LHO to make a damaging lead-directing double. For example, LHO may have a spade holding such as A-x or K-x.

The actual auction gives you the chance to make a descriptive bid: a raise to Three Diamonds shows both your game invitational values and your diamond fit. If partner has a little extra and a spade stopper, surely he can pot 3NT. *Do not cue-bid the enemy suit when you want to avoid a lead-directing double*.

On occasion, a lack of values may constrain your options. Calling their suit tends to increase the bidding level, so suggests high cards. Without them, you may have to make a simple bid and hope that things turn out for the best.

♠ K 7 6 5	YOU	LHO	PARTNER	RHO
♡ Q 8 4 3	–	1♢	Double	Pass
♢ 10 6 4	?			
♣ 7 2				

Should you choose hearts or spades? Of course, a cue bid of opener's suit will suggest two places to play and then partner will pick his better major and you will always find your best fit, will you not?

In itself, this is true, but think more deeply . . .

Earlier in this chapter, we examined numerous situations in which you could use a cue bid to show values (e.g., a constructive raise or a game try). Surely, it makes sense, therefore, that you cannot try the same trick when you lack the required values.

Making a Two Diamond cue bid in response to the takeout double establishes a forcing sequence. Partner will tell you his best major, yes, but he will see no need to jump when he holds a monster. He will expect you to find another bid, so cue-bidding and then passing when he bids a major may double-cross him. We recommend that you settle for 1♠. If you have game on, partner will bid again and you may get the chance to bid hearts; if either opponent competes with two of a minor, you can follow up with 2♡, letting partner choose a major at the two level. *Do not cue-bid the enemy suit when you lack the values for creating a force*.

♠ Q 6 4 2	YOU	LHO	PARTNER	RHO
♡ 8 7 6	–	1♡	1♠	Pass
♢ A K J 8 2	3♢			
♣ 3				

Remember what we said earlier about descriptive bids. Yes, a Two Heart cue bid would promise a constructive (or better) spade raise, but it would say very little else.

If fit-showing jumps feature in your system, you can give partner a much more accurate picture of this hand – game invitational values, 4-card spade support and a good diamond suit. This sounds perfect!

You should, however, note that not everyone plays fit-showing jumps, so you must check with your partner first. *Do not cue-bid the enemy suit when you should be showing a secondary suit*.

♠ A Q 10 7 6	YOU	LHO	PARTNER	RHO
♡ A Q J 4 2	–	–	–	1♣
◇ 7 3	1♠			
♣ 4				

Earlier in this chapter, we gave you a hand with 5-5 in the majors and said a Michaels Cue bid was the best way to describe it. Indeed some people use this convention on all hands with the right shape. However, a popular treatment is to reserve the cue bid for weak or strong hands. Let us explain. With clear extras, you plan to compete further, and on a minimum, you intend to pass unless partner invites you to go on. By contrast, if you have intermediate strength, you may face an awkward decision about what to do on the next round. You avoid this problem by starting with a simple overcall. *Do not cue-bid the enemy suit when your values are wrong for a two-suited bid*.

♠ K 10 6 4	YOU	LHO	PARTNER	RHO
♡ A	–	3◇	3♠	Pass
◇ 7 4	?			
♣ A K J 10 6 4				

When you first learned the game, you were probably taught that jumps and/or voluntary raises to the 5-level when your side has agreed a major ask partner to advance to a slam with good trumps. As a result, we suggest you check with your regular partner before unleashing our next proposal at the table.

If you think about it carefully, there are actually two spare bids at the 5-level: 5 of your major and 5 of the enemy suit.

Experts use a jump to Five Spades in an auction like this to make a slam try and to warn of two losers in the opponent's suit. If partner has the relevant control (diamonds on this auction), he must go on. The accepted responses are a cue bid with first-round control, six of the agreed suit with a singleton, and 5NT with the guarded king.

One can easily see the usefulness of this treatment. For a start, if you play Roman Key-Card Blackwood, you can find out all about partner's trumps via that route. If that will not answer the question satisfactorily, you could use a 5-level cue bid of the enemy's suit to ask partner about trumps as in the old-fashioned manner. *Do not cue-bid the enemy suit when you want to ask for a control in it*.

Golden Rule Four:

Cue-Bidding the Enemy Suit can

. . . Announce general values;
. . . Allow you to explore several spots;
. . . Distinguish your hand from a pre-emptive raise;
. . . Indicate a shortage in it;
. . . Ask for a full or half stopper for 3NT;
. . . Denote a control in it for slam purposes;
. . . Show two suits at once;
. . . Save you from having to jump to show strength;
. . . Imply two places to play;
. . . Express doubt about a stopper already shown;
. . . Announce a solid suit elsewhere (via a jump);
. . . Indicate values in one of two enemy suits;
. . . Expose a psyche.

Do not Cue-Bid the Enemy suit when

. . . Partner may incorrectly interpret it as natural;
. . . You have a clear alternative;
. . . You want to avoid a lead-directing double;
. . . You lack the values for creating a force;
. . . You should be showing a secondary suit;
. . . Your values are wrong for a two-suited bid;
. . . You want to ask for a control in it.

Rule Five: Pre-empt to the Limit

Pre-emptive bids make life difficult for your opponents, and the higher you pre-empt the less likely they are to guess right. In the early days, everyone stuck to what became known as the rule of 500: if you were doubled and partner turned up with a bust, you would lose that much. This broadly equates to the value of an enemy game.

Over the years, people have relaxed the requirements. If partner really holds nothing, the other side should have a slam. So you can afford to go down more. Quite how adventurously you bid depends on your philosophy and sense of adventure. You need to bear in mind that on occasion your opponents are going to fix you. Knowing when and how high to pre-empt allows you to get your own back.

Traditionally, a 3-level opening pre-empt shows a 7-card suit . . .

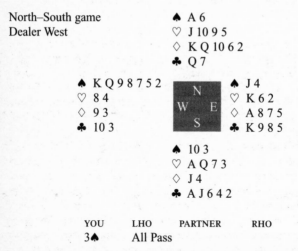

North–South game
Dealer West

♠ A 6
♡ J 10 9 5
◇ K Q 10 6 2
♣ Q 7

♠ K Q 9 8 7 5 2
♡ 8 4
◇ 9 3
♣ 10 3

♠ J 4
♡ K 6 2
◇ A 8 7 5
♣ K 9 8 5

♠ 10 3
♡ A Q 7 3
◇ J 4
♣ A J 6 4 2

YOU	LHO	PARTNER	RHO
3♠	All Pass		

With the North/South strength evenly divided and neither player holding much distribution your pre-empt figures to buy the auction. Not only do the opponents miss their making game in a red suit or 3NT, but you escape undoubled in Three Spades. You will quietly go two down and concede 100: a cheap price to pay compared to their game. ***Pre-empting to the limit can shut the opposition out.***

♠ 3	YOU	PARTNER	♠ A 10 4
♡ 7 4	3◇	3NT	♡ A 8 6
◇ K Q 10 6 5 4 3			◇ A 7 2
♣ Q 8 4			♣ J 10 6 2

Pre-emptive openings can also prove useful offensive weapons. Although he holds only 13 HCP and your opening at the three level promises a maximum of around nine, partner can virtually count nine tricks in a no-trump game: seven diamonds and two aces.

♠ Q 10 7 6 5	♠ A K 8 3 2
♡ 5	♡ A 7 3
◇ J 7 2	◇ Q 10 4
♣ A 8 6 4	♣ 3 2

YOU	LHO	PARTNER	RHO
–	1♣	1♠	Pass
4♠			

When the bidding reaches you on the first round of the auction, you have no real idea of who can make what. Can the opponents make game or even slam? Who holds the hearts? Will 4♠ be on?

The answer to all of these questions is that you do not care. With at least ten spades between you, your side should strive hard to play the hand. You must therefore take up as much bidding space as you safely can. How high is that, you may wonder . . .

Holding five-card spade support you should bid Four Spades. This offers something of a two-way bet. By going straight to game you leave the enemy guessing whether to bid on or to double. Moreover, unsure who owns the hand, they may let you escape undoubled when partner holds a minimum overcall. In practice, he has enough for a sound opening bid and the boot lies on the other foot. By going directly to game, you make it almost impossible for them to find a paying sacrifice. On deals like this, you must attach great importance to playing the hand and, ideally, at your choice of level. Pre-empting as high as you dare at your earliest opportunity greatly enhances your chances of achieving this objective. ***Pre-empting to the limit can help you find your own best contract.***

Love All
Dealer West

♠ J 10
♡ A 8 5 3 2
◇ A J 9
♣ K 10 3

♠ 8
♡ J
◇ K Q 8 7 6 5 4 2
♣ J 8 7

♠ K Q 6 5
♡ Q 10 7 4
◇ 10
♣ Q 6 5 2

♠ A 9 7 4 3 2
♡ K 9 6
◇ 3
♣ A 9 4

YOU	LHO	PARTNER	RHO
3◇	Pass	Pass	3♠
4◇	Double		

For a change, we have illustrated the sequence that you should never follow. You can see why . . .

On the first round, North lacks a suitable bid. He can hardly overcall on such a poor suit and nor can he make a take-out double with a doubleton spade or punt 3NT with only 13 points. Luckily for him, in the protective position South has an easy Three Spade overcall. He no doubt plans to call 3NT over this, but your Four Diamond rebid gives him fielder's choice. He could bid Four Spades, which is cold for an overtrick on careful play. In practice, he does better to double you. For one thing, if South turns up with only five spades and trumps break 5-1 (certainly possible on this auction), the spade game may easily fail. For another, he sees a reasonable hope of defeating your contract by more than the value of game. Indeed, if the defenders avoid opening up the clubs or conceding a trick to dummy's spades, they collect 800.

If you open 4◇, it works out totally differently. Obviously North passes and South may do too. Okay, he has six spades and one diamond; all the same, his aces and kings look good defensively and his spade spots are iffy. An expert panel might vote narrowly for 4♠, but a significant number of players would allow you to buy it in 4◇.
Pre-empting to the limit can give the enemy only one chance.

We saw on the previous hand how pushing the level one higher can make a crucial difference. Similarly, a single raise of partner's pre-empt can prove a most effective action. Suppose you hold:

♠ 8 5 3
♡ 10 7 2
♢ A J 9 5
♣ K 10 6

Whatever suit partner opens, you should give him a single raise of his weak two or three-level opening – or at any rate you will do so when non-vulnerable. Consider this from the opposing viewpoint:

♠ Q J 10 6 2
♡ A K 9 6 4 3
♢ –
♣ J 7

A Three Diamond opening by LHO passed round scarcely poses a problem: you cue-bid 4♢ asking partner to pick a major. However, if RHO has stolen your cue bid, you can no longer do that. You could double 4♢ and risk that partner decides to pass or, shock horror, bid 5♣. Alternatively, you could pot 4♡, which could go equally wrong.
    Likewise:

♠ A K 9 7 4
♡ Q J 8 5
♢ Q 10 7
♣ 8

Suppose LHO opens 3♣, partner overcalls 3♢ and RHO passes. In this sequence a forcing 3♠ fits the bill perfectly, allowing you to explore the possibility of playing in 4♠, 5♢ or 3NT.
    Now imagine RHO instead of passing raises to 4♣. You can hardly punt 4♠ on a 5-card suit. Therefore, your options consist of a catch-all double, praying partner does the right thing, or jumping to 5♢, which may have three quick losers. Forced to guess, you are bound to guess wrong some of the time. ***Pre-empting to the limit can increase the pressure on the opposition***.

Game All
Dealer East

```
                        ♠ 8 3 2
                        ♡ K 10 8 5 2
                        ◇ K J 5
                        ♣ 10 3
        ♠ A K 7 6                       ♠ Q J 10 5 4
        ♡ 9 3            N              ♡ 7 6
        ◇ 7 6 4 3     W     E           ◇ A 8
        ♣ J 7 2          S              ♣ A Q 8 5
                        ♠ 9
                        ♡ A Q J 4
                        ◇ Q 10 9 2
                        ♣ K 9 6 4
```

YOU	LHO	PARTNER	RHO
–	–	1♠	Double
3♠			

For many years it has been accepted that after an opponent makes a take-out double you should raise partner to one level higher than you would without the double. On a very weak hand you can bid Two Spades – and on a hand where you would normally make a simple raise you now jump. Let us examine the theory behind this.

With the law of total tricks, the total number of tricks available for contracts both ways equates to the total number of trumps each side holds. Put another way, if your side has nine spades and they have nine hearts, there should be eighteen tricks available between spade and heart contracts. Thus, if the high cards split equally, both Three Spades and Three Hearts will make. On the basis that when you have a fit, the other side normally has one of similar length, you can safely reckon to bid to the level equal to the number of trumps your side holds. Here, you surely hold at least nine trumps, so you can afford to contract for nine tricks. You should, therefore, jump to Three Spades. Whether this makes or not is probably irrelevant – if you cannot make a part-score in your long suit, the opponents may well have game available in theirs. Moreover, they might just bid it if you give them room to investigate. Here the deal plays one trick better than the law suggests, with 3♠ and 4♡ both on. This makes it all the more vital to buy the contract. ***Pre-empting to the limit can get you directly to your safe total tricks level***.

Game All
Dealer East

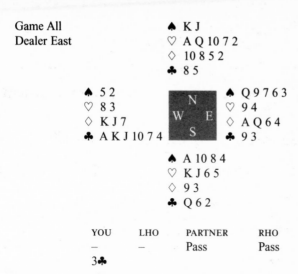

```
                    ♠ K J
                    ♡ A Q 10 7 2
                    ◇ 10 8 5 2
                    ♣ 8 5
    ♠ 5 2                              ♠ Q 9 7 6 3
    ♡ 8 3              N               ♡ 9 4
    ◇ K J 7       W         E          ◇ A Q 6 4
    ♣ A K J 10 7 4        S            ♣ 9 3
                    ♠ A 10 8 4
                    ♡ K J 6 5
                    ◇ 9 3
                    ♣ Q 6 2
```

YOU	LHO	PARTNER	RHO
–	–	Pass	Pass
3♣			

After two passes, you know that the opponents have about half of the high cards (or more). Your major-suit holdings should therefore ring alarm bells because the other side is very likely to possess a fit in one or both majors. This will enable them to outbid your clubs.

If you open One Club and the layout turns out as shown here, North will come in with a One Heart overcall and the enemy will get to Three Hearts: minus 140 for your side.

Facing a passed partner, your game prospects appear minimal, so you should be prepared to pre-empt despite 12 HCP. Your reward here comes via a winning club finesse and Three Clubs makes.

If a very aggressive North does find a 3♡ overcall, your heavy pre-empt will still score a goal: South can hardly fail to raise, and your side will cash four top winners to beat the game. ***Pre-empting to the limit can let you steal the contract.***

You can also take advantage of partner's passed hand status by making heavy pre-emptive overcalls. If you judge that your side stands little hope of making game, and an opposing opening bid will tend to increase the likelihood of this, you can afford to fool partner. You can deceive many opponents with this tactic. They place you with a weak hand for your action and know that partner's inability to open limits his values. They then conclude they have game on their way – wrong!

♠ A 8 7 6 4 2	YOU	LHO	PARTNER	RHO
♡ 10 7 4	?			
◇ A 6				
♣ 4 2				

Even if you play Weak Twos (or a Multi), you should still pass with this hand as dealer. With your pair of aces and moderate suit, your hand is not sufficiently offensively orientated.

A pre-emptive bid suggests good playing strength (with your long suit as trumps) and relatively poor defensive values. Pre-empting on a hand such as this one can mislead partner in a number of ways. For example, he might make a phantom sacrifice. Alternatively, he might decide against doubling the opponents for fear that you can offer little defensive help, and thus your side will miss out on a juicy penalty. You might also miss a good game or slam when your side belongs in something other than spades. ***Do not pre-empt to the limit when you have a good hand defensively.***

♠ K 10 9 5	YOU	PARTNER	♠ A Q J 4 3
♡ 6 5	?		♡ A J 7
◇ A J 10 7 4 3 2			◇ 5
♣ –			♣ Q 8 6 3

In the early days of bidding, making a pre-emptive opening with four-card support for an unbid major was a complete no-no. Now some experts take the view that as most of the time you miss a fit in another suit it bears little consequence. If the other side is going to outbid you, what does it matter if you fail to locate your best fit? However, even this permissive school puts limits on outside shape and values. Here you hold a fantastic hand in support of spades: king of trumps, ace of diamonds and, with your void, great ruffing potential. If you open Three Diamonds, you may play there with a game or slam on in spades. Remember, a pass as dealer still allows you to give the opponents a hard time later. Indeed, it gives you carte blanche to bid a lot without exciting partner. If he fails to open in third seat, you will compete vigorously on the next round. ***Do not pre-empt to the limit when your hand offers potential support for partner.***

```
♠ 6 2              YOU        PARTNER
♡ J 9 7 6 4 3 2    ?
◇ K 4
♣ Q 7
```

With a 7-card suit, you would normally open at the 3-level – if partner turns up with a third of the remaining six hearts, you will have a nine-card fit, enough for the 3-level as we saw on page 62. On a hand such as this one, though, your suit is poor and you possess defensive values outside. Opening Three Hearts will sometimes work, but it also severely risks leading partner astray. For example, he might lead a heart from K-x or try a sacrifice that costs too much.

Fortunately, if you play Weak Twos (or a Multi), a compromise exists. If you wish to take some positive action on this hand, you could open with a 2-level pre-empt. *Do not pre-empt to the limit when your long suit is poor*.

```
♠ A K Q J 10 9 6   YOU     PARTNER    ♠ 8 2
♡ K                1♠      2◇          ♡ J 7 4
◇ 8 7 3            3♠      4♣          ◇ A K Q J 4
♣ J 6              4♡      4NT         ♣ A 9 4
                   5♠      6♠
```

In some ways, the West hand appears suitable for a four-level opening. For sure, you expect to take far more tricks with spades as trumps than you do against some opposing contract. You can count on seven tricks offensively and you might score only one defending. However, the arguments against strike us as compelling. Firstly, holding long spades reduces the danger of being kept out of the later bidding or running into an opposing sacrifice. Secondly, if partner has moderate values but few spades, you would be pre-empting yourself out of your own part-score. Thirdly, you possess too many controls to make what amounts to a shut-out bid.

Surely you agree that the above sequence to 6♠, using a couple of cue bids (4♣ and 4♡) then Roman Key-Card Blackwood, sounds much more effective than hearing partner pass out 4♠. After all, if he fears that you might hold ace-queen-jack to eight spades and two low hearts, he can hardly feel safe at the five level. *Do not pre-empt to the limit when staying low could lead to better things*.

		YOU	LHO	PARTNER	RHO
♠	7 3	YOU	LHO	PARTNER	RHO
♡	A Q 8 7 6 5	–	Pass	Pass	Pass
◇	Q 9 4	?			
♣	10 2				

We hope you would not consider opening a Weak Two on this. Just show gratitude that you can pass out a hand on which, in all probability, the opponents have both the balance of the high cards and the spade suit.

In fourth position, the range for a Weak Two should be something like 10-12. Thus, you can describe a minimum opening bid including a good 6-card suit without allowing the opponents an easy route into the auction.

A secondary advantage of such an agreement is that when partner opens at the 1-level in fourth seat and then rebids his suit, you can assume he has better than a minimum opening bid. ***Do not pre-empt to the limit when you are in the pass-out seat***.

Golden Rule Five:

Pre-empting to the Limit can

. . . Shut the opposition out;
. . . Help you find your own best contract;
. . . Give the enemy only one chance;
. . . Increase the pressure on the opposition;
. . . Get you directly to your safe total tricks level;
. . . Let you steal the contract.

Do not Pre-empt to the Limit when

. . . You have a good hand defensively;
. . . Your hand offers potential support for partner;
. . . Your long suit is poor;
. . . Staying low may lead to better things;
. . . You are in the pass-out seat.

Rule Six: Tread Warily after Their Pre-empt

Bidding over an opponent's opening pre-emptive bid will often lead to a poor result. For a start, his partner may lie waiting for you with a juicy penalty double. Even if that fails to happen, partner may carry you too high, or a lack of bidding space may cause you to miss your best fit. There is also considerable scope for misunderstanding in crowded auctions: 'Is 4NT Blackwood or natural in this auction?' or 'Does partner's change of suit show a suit or does he intend it as a cue bid agreeing mine?' etc.

Passing carries its risks too. Multiple World Champion Bobby Wolff once made a comment that the fact that bidding is dangerous is not a reason for passing a pre-empt. How often do you sell out to a pre-emptive opening only to find that your side had game available?

The fact that one opponent holds a long suit increases the chance that your side possesses a fit. However, your high cards are not worth more just because one opponent has pre-empted. Indeed, the greater likelihood of bad breaks may marginally reduce their value.

Essentially, pre-empts make you guess. You will not guess right every time. Even the world's best players would admit to an imperfect record in these situations. Still, you can hope to get more of these decisions right than you get wrong. After an opposing pre-emptive opening, the accepted advice is to act on the basis that partner has roughly eight HCP. As usual, we start with cases obeying the rule.

♠ K 7 6	♠ A Q 10 8 3 2
♡ J 7 2	♡ A 4
◇ 9 4 3	◇ A 2
♣ K 8 6 5	♣ 10 4 2

YOU	LHO	PARTNER	RHO
–	3◇	3♠	Pass
?			

Take a quick look at the hand for partner's overcall. Clearly, he cannot underwrite nine tricks on his own, and yet most experienced players would consider the overcall routine. The reason for this is that they hope to find a smattering of high cards opposite.

Now the problem moves around the table to you. You have a fit for partner's suit and more high cards than you might (you might hold a Yarborough for all he knows). Should you, therefore, raise to game?

Actually, your hand appears fractionally worse than what partner was envisaging when he came in at the 3-level. As we mentioned above, he will normally act on the assumption that you will hold about 8 HCP. Therefore, your 7-count rates as slightly sub-minimum. There is also a reasonable expectation that you would hold three trumps. (With seven spades missing and LHO predicted to have a shortage, on average both RHO and you will hold three.)

This means, as you can see, that you can offer nothing more than partner anticipated. Pass Three Spades and hope that he can come to nine tricks.

♠ K 10 3	♠ Q 6 4 2
♡ Q 7 4 2	♡ K 8 6 3
◇ K Q 5	◇ A J 10 7
♣ J 10 3	♣ 4

YOU	LHO	PARTNER	RHO
–	–	Pass	3♣
Pass	Pass	Double	Pass
?			

True, you hold eleven points rather than the eight you might think partner would feel entitled to hope for. Furthermore, you have little wasted in clubs. This all suggests aggression. Now what can you see as the arguments for a simple Three Heart response?

For a start, your 3-4-3-3 distribution will generate few winners. More importantly, partner failed to open, which limits his hand, and he is in the protective seat. Whilst you might have game values if he turns up with a void in clubs, the odds appear against it. Far more likely, partner is doubling to compete the part-score and to allow for the possibility that you wish to pass for penalties.

Finally, suppose that LHO had dealt and opened Three Clubs and partner had doubled. You would then just be worth a non-minimum call. With such poor shape, you would need nearly all these high cards to justify making one. *Treading warily after their pre-empt can allow partner some leeway.*

```
    ♠ A Q 10 6 4        ♠ 8 7 3
    ♡ 10                ♡ Q J 3
    ◇ A K 7             ◇ Q 10 5 2
    ♣ K 10 7 4          ♣ Q 9 3
```

YOU	LHO	PARTNER	RHO
–	–	–	4♡
Double			

If the opponents had passed throughout, you might have found your way into 4♠. It would then have been a marginal contract but, after a pre-empt, all of the suits figure to break poorly. Moreover, LHO will probably turn up with both length and strength in spades over you. In the present scenario, Four Spades sounds very much odds against. You do much better to double Four Hearts, giving partner the option to defend. He will take you up on this with these cards.

```
    ♠ Q 8 6 4           ♠ A J 5 2
    ♡ 6 3               ♡ A 7
    ◇ K J               ◇ Q 8 4 2
    ♣ A Q 8 6 3         ♣ J 5 4
```

YOU	LHO	PARTNER	RHO
1♣	1♡	Double	4♡
?			

A cursory analysis of how this pair of hands might fare in Four Spades suggests you will lose a trick in each suit unless North holds K-x of spades or South K-x of clubs. Unfortunately, if one of the black suits breaks 4-1, finding a friendly layout of the other may prove of no avail. Given the vigorous opposing bidding, it seems extremely probable that someone holds a black-suit singleton. This means you want to play for four tricks rather than ten. You ought also to be able to work this out from the fact that partner's negative double will rarely contain five spades. If you can make ten tricks on an 8-card fit, you should do well enough defending. You should pass over RHO's Four Hearts and pass again if, as will happen here, partner follows up with a second double to show extra values. ***Treading warily after their pre-empt can take account of bad breaks***.

East– West game
Dealer South

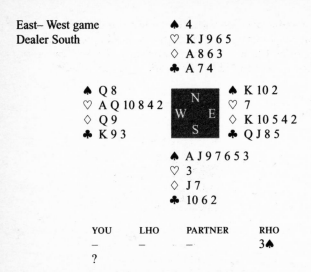

```
                    ♠ 4
                    ♡ K J 9 6 5
                    ◇ A 8 6 3
                    ♣ A 7 4
   ♠ Q 8                          ♠ K 10 2
   ♡ A Q 10 8 4 2    N            ♡ 7
   ◇ Q 9          W     E         ◇ K 10 5 4 2
   ♣ K 9 3           S            ♣ Q J 8 5
                    ♠ A J 9 7 6 5 3
                    ♡ 3
                    ◇ J 7
                    ♣ 10 6 2
```

YOU	LHO	PARTNER	RHO
–	–	–	3♠
?			

Yes, you have an opening bid and a decent 6-card major. Do you, therefore, feel worried that passing at this point will let the opponents steal the hand when your side can make an easy game?

Occasionally, that will happen – partner will produce the perfect hand for you but be unable to come in. One way to see whether bidding seems sensible is to ask yourself if you would have driven to game in an unopposed auction in which you opened One Heart and partner responded 1NT. Of course you would not do so, and yet now you are contemplating bidding that game facing the same expected balanced 8-count.

If you remain unconvinced, write down a half dozen hands with 8 HCP – i.e., just the type of hand you picture partner to hold. Facing how many of them do you want to declare Four Hearts? Unless he produces a useful shortage, at the very best game would appear to depend on two finesses as well as reasonable breaks.

There is one more factor to consider. On the actual deal shown, LHO will be delighted to double if you venture an overcall. We have been kind enough to spare you from a ruff by South, the short trump hand, but the resulting penalty will still cause you grief, particularly if you need to explain it to team-mates. *Treading warily after their pre-empt can avoid a double by the other opponent.*

Up until now, the question has generally been whether to bid at all over their pre-empt rather than how high you should go. Fortunately, you will sometimes have more than sufficient to act and you must consider whether to go for a slam or to settle for a game contract.

East–West game
Dealer North

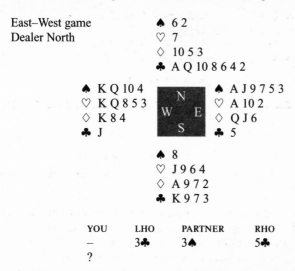

```
                    ♠ 6 2
                    ♡ 7
                    ♢ 10 5 3
                    ♣ A Q 10 8 6 4 2
     ♠ K Q 10 4              ♠ A J 9 7 5 3
     ♡ K Q 8 5 3     N       ♡ A 10 2
     ♢ K 8 4     W     E     ♢ Q J 6
     ♣ J            S        ♣ 5
                    ♠ 8
                    ♡ J 9 6 4
                    ♢ A 9 7 2
                    ♣ K 9 7 3
```

YOU	LHO	PARTNER	RHO
–	3♣	3♠	5♣
?			

You can tell the deal belongs to your side and that the opponents are sacrificing, but partner is not in on the secret. From his viewpoint, RHO could be bidding to make and you might hold next to nothing. This rules out a pass in the hope partner reads it as forcing. Your options consist of a simple Five Spades, a gambling Six Spades, or a value-showing double. One can easily exclude the double. How could partner fathom that you have such good support for his suit?

If partner holds three aces, you surely want to reach Six Spades, but if he has only two, you want to stop in five. You cannot easily tell, but the threat of a seven-level sacrifice gives you reason to exercise caution. If you can make Six Spades, the opponents will bid Seven Clubs and you may pick up about 800; if not, presumably because they both hold an ace, they will defend and you will lose 100. This means that you stand to gain very little by potting a slam. Just settle for Five Spades. You will probably score 650 (or 680) because the enemy will be afraid a sacrifice might push you into a slam. ***Treading warily after their pre-empt can save you from taking a needless risk.***

```
♠ K 3 2          ♠ Q J 7
♡ A 10 6         ♡ Q 4
♦ Q 10 5         ♦ K 8 3 2
♣ K Q 7 4        ♣ 8 6 5 2
```

YOU	LHO	PARTNER	RHO
–	3♡	Pass	Pass
?			

This time it seems close. There are 8-HCP hands for partner on which 3NT might make – if he has a good 5-card suit, perhaps.

Nevertheless, your sterile 3-3-3-4 reduces your playing strength, whilst increasing the prospects you can beat Three Hearts. If partner turns up with much less than his projected 8 HCP, bidding 3NT could result in a bloodbath. There are times to act bravely, but not on this deal. Selling out rates to win hands down. ***Treading warily after their pre-empt can stop you from turning a plus into a minus***.

```
♠ J 9 6 4        ♠ Q 10 7 2
♡ –              ♡ Q 10 6 4
♦ A J 8 6 5      ♦ K 10 3
♣ K J 9 2        ♣ A 4
```

YOU	LHO	PARTNER	RHO
–	2♡ *	Pass	Pass
?			

You should always think twice before making a takeout double with a void in the enemy's suit. The reason for this is that your void increases the likelihood partner will turn up with a trump holding on which he will elect to defend. In that case, things will usually go better for your side if you have a trump to lead through declarer. However, allowing the opponents to steal the auction when you hold so much offensive potential is losing bridge. Therefore, you have to double.

One other factor is that partner will only leave in a take-out double at the 2-level with at least five decent trumps. Doing so on this East hand would be foolhardy. In practice, he will bid Three Spades, which you will probably pass. ***Bid up after their pre-empt when your shape and the bidding level allow safe entry***.

```
        ♠ Q 8            ♠ K 7 5 3
        ♡ K Q J 10 9 6 5  ♡ 8 4
        ◇ K J 7          ◇ A 10 3 2
        ♣ 5              ♣ J 6 2
```

YOU	LHO	PARTNER	RHO
–	–	–	4♣
?			

As you no doubt already worked out, high-card points are only one factor in judging a hand's true value. Suit quality and playing strength also play a vital part, particularly in high-level competitive auctions.

This West hand may contain only 12 HCP, but you are unlikely to come across a clearer example of an automatic 4-level overcall. Game will represent an excellent proposition if you find partner with a couple of high cards outside RHO's suit.

The East hand shown here illustrates the true potential of this West hand – you possess a combined 20 HCP (including a useless jack) and yet game has great chances. *Bid up after their pre-empt when a fair share from partner will let your contract make*.

```
        ♠ A J 10 8 7 4   ♠ 9 2
        ♡ 7 6 5          ♡ 10
        ◇ 7 3            ◇ A K 8 4
        ♣ K 4            ♣ A Q J 9 7 5
```

YOU	LHO	PARTNER	RHO
–	2♡ *	3♣	4♡
?			

In an uncontested auction, you can use conventions like splinter bids to uncover hands that fit well. In competitive auctions, you will often be able to picture partner's hand from the enemy bidding.

Here, you can deduce the heart shortage in partner's hand. As a result, you can confidently predict that the hands will fit well and you should bid Four Spades. Indeed, you might count yourself unlucky that partner tables only a doubleton trump. Even so, prospects for game in spades still appear very good. *Bid up after their pre-empt when the opposing fit marks partner with shortness*.

The fact that one opponent holds a weak hand with a long suit can often turn out to your advantage. For example, a judicious hold-up (particularly in a no-trump contract) can keep the pre-emptor off play. Remember, too, that the partner of the pre-emptor will be long and strong in the other suits, rendering him susceptible to a throw-in or a squeeze. Even finesses in the other suits stand a better than usual chance of working if they go into the hand with the long suit.

Game All   ♠ Q 4
Dealer East   ♡ Q 9 8 6 5
                       ♦ K 6
                       ♣ A 9 7 2

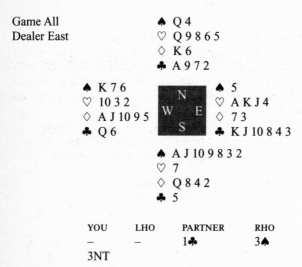

	♠ K 7 6	♠ 5
	♡ 10 3 2	♡ A K J 4
	◇ A J 10 9 5	◇ 7 3
	♣ Q 6	♣ K J 10 8 4 3

                   ♠ A J 10 9 8 3 2
                   ♡ 7
                   ◇ Q 8 4 2
                   ♣ 5

YOU	LHO	PARTNER	RHO
–	–	1♣	3♠
3NT			

Looking at just the East/West cards, you would conclude that any game contract rates to fail if North/South defend accurately. If you add South's pre-emptive overcall to the mix, though, one can easily imagine how a no-trump game may prove unbeatable.

Suddenly, the spade suit, the lead of which would have spelled instant defeat if the North/South cards in the suit divided 5-4, can be nullified by a simple duck of the first round. This stands a particularly good chance of working since South's pre-empt makes it odds on that he will not hold the club ace as an entry to his winners. Of course, partner might turn up without such good clubs, but then you know that you could take any diamond finesses into LHO. *Bid up after their pre-empt when knowing about bad breaks helps you*.

	♠ Q 9 4	♠ J 8 2
	♡ A 5	♡ K 10
	◇ K J 10 9	◇ A 7 5 4
	♣ J 10 9 7	♣ A 8 6 2

YOU	LHO	PARTNER	RHO
–	–	1NT(12-14)	3♡
3NT			

Holding good spot cards assumes added importance when suits rate to break unevenly. For example, the excellent intermediates in the minor suits here will enable you to score seven tricks in those suits even if North (as anticipated) holds at least four cards in one or both. Indeed, holding the ten and nine of both key suits may very well prove the difference between making eight tricks and nine.

If you counted just your high-card points, bidding game opposite a weak no-trump opening would be a very marginal decision. The good intermediate cards should sway the decision towards aggression.

	♠ 6	♠ K 7
	♡ A Q J 9 8 6 5 2	♡ 10 4
	◇ A 7 4	◇ K 10 6 5
	♣ 6	♣ K 9 5 4 2

YOU	LHO	PARTNER	RHO
1♡	4♠	Double	Pass
?			

When you opened One Heart, partner knew little about your hand other than that you had enough for an opening bid and that you held at least four hearts (five if you use five-card majors). In fact, you hold an 8-card suit, at least three more hearts than partner has any right to expect. This gives you hugely more playing strength than he could reasonably envisage. If RHO holds the king of hearts and partner has enough hearts (and entries) for you to finesse, you can make nine tricks on your own with hearts as trumps. If partner can contribute a couple of winners, you will make Five Hearts. If not, Four Spades might scrape home and you still want to bid Five Hearts. **Bid up after their pre-empt when your trumps or spot cards are good**.

		YOU	LHO	PARTNER	RHO
♠ A Q 6		1♡	3♣	3♡	Pass
♡ A K 9 7 5		?			
◇ K J 7					
♣ J 6					

In this situation, partner's raise means something different from what it would have done if LHO had passed. Most probably, he would have bid only Two Hearts. In that situation, you would very likely have made a game try. Now you lack any space to do that. Whilst you cannot guarantee making ten tricks, it makes sense to press on to game. For one thing, with a marginal raise to Two Hearts, partner could have passed waiting for you to re-open. For another, the lure of a game bonus means you stand to gain more if you call Four Hearts and are right. ***Bid up after their pre-empt when you are good for your previous bidding***.

Golden Rule Six:

Treading Warily after Their Pre-empt can

. . . Allow partner some leeway;
. . . Take account of bad breaks;
. . . Avoid a double by the other opponent;
. . . Save you from taking a needless risk;
. . . Stop you from turning a plus into a minus.

Bid up after Their Pre-empt when

. . . Your shape and the bidding level allow safe entry;
. . . A fair share from partner will let your contract make;
. . . The opposing fit marks partner with shortness;
. . . Knowing about bad breaks helps you;
. . . Your trumps or spot cards are good;
. . . You are good for your previous bidding.

Rule Seven: Be Cautious in Save Situations

Even before the 1987 change to duplicate scores for non-vulnerable multiple undertricks, sacrificing was a hazardous affair. If you bid over an opponent's contract when expecting to go down yourself, you take on several risks. Firstly, the penalty might cost more than their contract; secondly, their contract might have gone down; finally they might find a better spot. Furthermore, depending upon other results on the board, what looks like a cheap sacrifice may show little profit.

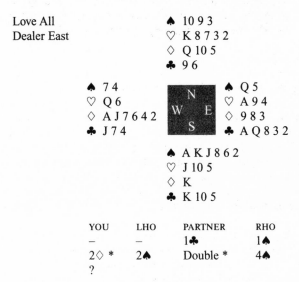

Love All
Dealer East

♠ 10 9 3
♡ K 8 7 3 2
◇ Q 10 5
♣ 9 6

♠ 7 4
♡ Q 6
◇ A J 7 6 4 2
♣ J 7 4

♠ Q 5
♡ A 9 4
◇ 9 8 3
♣ A Q 8 3 2

♠ A K J 8 6 2
♡ J 10 5
◇ K
♣ K 10 5

YOU	LHO	PARTNER	RHO
–	–	1♣	1♠
2◇ *	2♠	Double *	4♠
?			

In this sequence partner's One Club opening was natural, your 'disturbed' Two Diamonds response was non-forcing and partner's double showed three-card diamond support.

Sure, you possess 3-card club support you have yet to show and partner says he holds three trumps for you. However, it could prove unwise to back in at the five level, perhaps via 4NT. You have holes in both minors and this 2-2 in the majors is bad. As the cards lie, you would concede a punitive 800 if someone doubles. ***Being cautious in save situations can protect you from going for a big number***.

Game All   ♠ A Q 8 7 2
Dealer North   ♡ 9 7 3
                 ◇ Q 2
                 ♣ A J 5

	♠ 6		♠ K 5 4
	♡ K Q 8 6		♡ 10 2
	◇ J 7 4 3		◇ A K 10 8 6 5
	♣ 10 7 4 2		♣ Q 8

            ♠ J 10 9 3
            ♡ A J 5 4
            ◇ 9
            ♣ K 9 6 3

YOU	LHO	PARTNER	RHO
–	1♠	2◇	4♠
?			

As we mentioned at the start of the chapter, a vital component in the process for evaluating a sacrifice involves assessing the chance that the opponent's contract might fail. On a good day, both your king and queen of hearts will take tricks – for example if RHO has the ace and partner is fairly short in the suit. It also sounds quite plausible that partner can contribute a few defensive tricks. After all, he made a vulnerable 2-level overcall. Your singleton spade suggests that if declarer needs a trump finesse or break, he will be unlucky; also, partner could easily come up with a trick in one or both minors.

With so many ways Four Spades might go down, you would only bid Five Diamonds if you saw a realistic chance of making it. This appears unlikely unless partner has a singleton club. Even then, the diamonds would need to play for no loser and he would need an ace on the side. Therefore you should pass. To justify bidding 5◇ with this combination of high cards you would want more shape, a fifth diamond or perhaps a void in spades. As things stand, you would certainly lose 500 in 5◇ doubled, and it could be worse – put partner with a club more and the ♡A offside and you might go for 800.

As the cards lie, declarer will do well to get out for one down in 4♠. In theory, he might lose two hearts, a spade, a diamond and a club, although he should avoid one of these losers. ***Being cautious in save situations can give you a chance of a plus score.***

North–South game
Dealer North

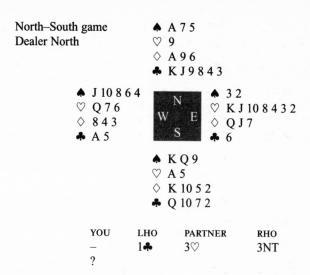

♠ A 7 5
♡ 9
◇ A 9 6
♣ K J 9 8 4 3

♠ J 10 8 6 4
♡ Q 7 6
◇ 8 4 3
♣ A 5

♠ 3 2
♡ K J 10 8 4 3 2
◇ Q J 7
♣ 6

♠ K Q 9
♡ A 5
◇ K 10 5 2
♣ Q 10 7 2

YOU	LHO	PARTNER	RHO
–	1♣	3♡	3NT
?			

Once you hear partner's 3♡, a weak pre-emptive bid, especially at this vulnerability, you may reckon the opponents can make a game or slam. You possess one defensive trick, and it would be a major surprise if partner has more than one. This might lead you to start pulling your 4♡ card out of your bidding box before you have thought through the other issues. We warn against this. If pre-emptive action by your side forces them to guess, you should take extra care before taking out a sacrifice; they may be in a sub-optimal spot.

Given your holding of Q-x-x, it seems highly likely declarer has only a single heart stopper. Moreover, unless this consists of A-x-x or K-J-x, he will have to use his stopper on the first or second round of the suit. This will leave you with a heart with which to continue when you get in with the ace of clubs. Declarer may have long diamonds, but if not, he will need to play on clubs and you will defeat him.

Do you see what will happen if you carelessly bid Four Hearts? North will pass to show an unbalanced hand; then South, aware of the heart weakness and knowing from his lack of aces that there are unlikely to be ten top tricks in no-trumps, will seize the opportunity to bid the laydown 5♣. True, you could profitably sacrifice in Five Hearts doubled and get out for 500, but surely you would rather keep open the option of a plus by score defending 3NT. *Being cautious in save situations can deter the enemy from finding a better spot.*

North–South game
Dealer East

```
North
♠ K 4
♡ J 3
◇ K 8 7 6 3
♣ K J 8 6

West                      East
♠ J 8 6 5 2               ♠ 9 7 3
♡ A 8 2                   ♡ K Q 10 7 6 5 4
◇ 5                       ◇ 9
♣ 9 4 3 2                 ♣ Q 7

South
♠ A Q 10
♡ 9
◇ A Q J 10 4 2
♣ A 10 5
```

YOU	LHO	PARTNER	RHO
–	–	3♡	4◇
4♡	5◇	Pass	6◇
?			

So far, each auction has sounded reasonably normal. You would anticipate that the other table (in a teams match) or the room (in a pairs event) might replicate it – or at any rate reach a similar stage with similar information on offer to the participants. On occasion, this state of affairs does not exist. If you study the bidding in the diagram, you may smell a rat. RHO makes a simple overcall, albeit at a high level, his partner advances to game, possibly stretching to compete against your Four Hearts, then RHO somehow finds a raise to slam.

Maybe some pairs will bid the same way, but you doubt that many will. Either the opponents hold tricky hands to bid or they have taken an ambitious view. Whichever way, it sounds like the field may stay out of 6◇. This being the case, you should only save in 6♡ if you believe both that their contract will make and that you can get out for less than the value of game. With your hand, you cannot really say this. If you sacrifice, you probably book yourself a miserable score. To stand a chance of obtaining a decent result you must defend. As the cards lie, declarer needs to guess the location of the club queen to make twelve tricks. Luckily for you, declarer can obtain an almost complete count on the hand, and finding you with more clubs than your partner, he will probably finesse the wrong way. ***Being cautious in save situations can avoid a near certain poor score.***

North–South game
Dealer East

♠ K 10 4
♡ 3
◇ Q J 10 8 5
♣ A 7 6 4

♠ 9 6 5 2
♡ K J 9 7 6
◇ 4
♣ K 9 3

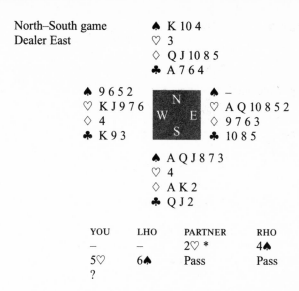

♠ –
♡ A Q 10 8 5 2
◇ 9 7 6 3
♣ 10 8 5

♠ A Q J 8 7 3
♡ 4
◇ A K 2
♣ Q J 2

YOU	LHO	PARTNER	RHO
–	–	2♡ *	4♠
5♡	6♠	Pass	Pass
?			

Even in quite a strong field, a fair proportion of pairs will tend to miss all but the most blindingly obvious of slam contracts. Likewise, when they have a grand slam, a good number of tables will see the auction grind to a halt at the six level. It follows that if you reserve your sacrificing for when you expect to lose less than the next rung down, you will earn more good scores and incur few disasters. At teams, similar thinking applies, although now you will tend to trust teammates to do the right thing. If you concede a penalty of 500 when the opponents call a slam, you will achieve a huge swing if teammates bid and make a slam. These big pick ups will compensate for the occasional phantom sacrifice. The small penalty scores will also protect your other pair if they have inexplicably missed the boat. For example, if they come back with +680, you gain 5 IMPs with –500. If, however, you were –1430, you would lose 13 IMPs. Therefore, your sacrifice gains 18 IMPs. This affords you more latitude.

Here you hold enough spades to place partner with a void, in which case you will have very few losers in a heart contract, most likely three or four. Whilst you must consider the possibility that someone will venture Seven Spades over Seven Hearts, you own enough defensive values to hope this may represent good news. ***Sacrificing can work well when you expect it to be dirt cheap.***

On the last four examples, your opponents alone were vulnerable. Whilst this scenario occurs on only one deal in four, it represents the most common vulnerability for successful sacrifices. You can afford to go 3 down if they have a game and at least 5 down if they have a slam. With equal vulnerability, either game all or love all, you need to be more circumspect. You can afford to go 2 down if they can make a game or 4 down if they can make slam, although ideally you want to plan to take an extra trick to allow a margin for error.

Game All   ♠ Q 3
Dealer West   ♡ A K 10 9 3
                     ◇ A Q 8 5
                     ♣ 8 7

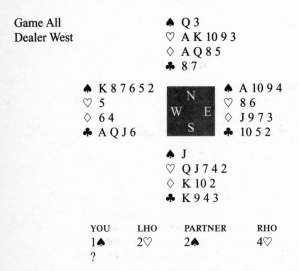

♠ K 8 7 6 5 2		♠ A 10 9 4
♡ 5	N	♡ 8 6
◇ 6 4	W E	◇ J 9 7 3
♣ A Q J 6	S	♣ 10 5 2

                 ♠ J
                 ♡ Q J 7 4 2
                 ◇ K 10 2
                 ♣ K 9 4 3

YOU	LHO	PARTNER	RHO
1♠	2♡	2♠	4♡
?			

After a single raise from partner, you would not normally bid game. We suppose you might try a pre-emptive re-raise to Three Spades if you play it that way, but certainly no more. After RHO's jump to Four Hearts, you need to reassess. Assuming one opponent turns up with a doubleton club and the other a singleton spade, you have one and a half defensive tricks. Partner's single raise will often contain only one defensive winner, so their game figures to make. Added to this, if partner produces a few right cards, you might actually make Four Spades. If he holds the spade ace and the club finesse works, you will need little more. Whatever he has, you would consider yourself unlucky to lose more than one trick in each major, two diamonds and a club. Thus, an 800 penalty seems out of the question. So bid 4♠. *Sacrificing can be very right if you might make your contract.*

In the hands to date, we have evaluated whether to sacrifice on the basis that, if you do so, the opponents will double. In practice, if they consider your action unusual, or they suspect that the penalty will provide inadequate recompense, they will often bid one more. When this means you push them from four into five of a major, you are often on to a good thing. Compared with playing at the four level, they score the same if they make 11 tricks but you do hugely better if they only manage 10. You should aim to exploit this.

North–South game
Dealer South

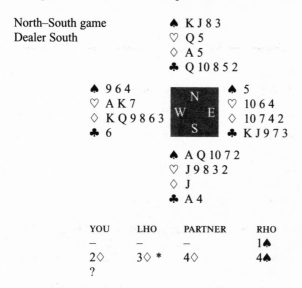

♠ K J 8 3
♡ Q 5
◇ A 5
♣ Q 10 8 5 2

♠ 9 6 4
♡ A K 7
◇ K Q 9 8 6 3
♣ 6

♠ 5
♡ 10 6 4
◇ 10 7 4 2
♣ K J 9 7 3

♠ A Q 10 7 2
♡ J 9 8 3 2
◇ J
♣ A 4

YOU	LHO	PARTNER	RHO
–	–	–	1♠
2◇	3◇ *	4◇	4♠
?			

You have fine solid values in the red suits, which give you good playing strength. In addition, your three low spades seem a pleasing feature. Partner probably holds a singleton, leaving you few losers there. You expect to get out for one or two down in Five Diamonds doubled and would be sorely disappointed if the sacrifice costs more than the opposing game. In practice, sensing they will not get rich from defending, one opponent or the other will probably go to Five Spades. This suits you nicely. Your two top hearts seem set to score and, if partner can contribute a defensive trick, they will go one down. Indeed this is precisely what happens. Declarer can discard three clubs from dummy on his long hearts but he still has to lose a club. ***Sacrificing can push your opposition a level higher.***

North–South game
Dealer North

♠ A K Q J 10 8 6
♡ A K 7
◇ 8
♣ 8 5

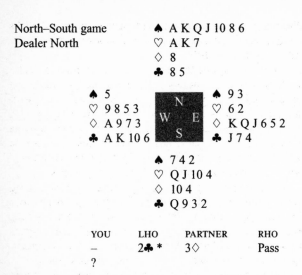

♠ 5
♡ 9 8 5 3
◇ A 9 7 3
♣ A K 10 6

♠ 9 3
♡ 6 2
◇ K Q J 6 5 2
♣ J 7 4

♠ 7 4 2
♡ Q J 10 4
◇ 10 4
♣ Q 9 3 2

YOU	LHO	PARTNER	RHO
–	2♣ *	3◇	Pass
?			

One of the best tactics to encourage the opponents to venture a level higher than they really want to go is to sacrifice before they reach their destination. You can exert the most pressure by bidding to the level where you want to be before they even manage to agree a suit. People with distributional hands they have yet to express, or with support for partner they have still to disclose, find it incredibly difficult to refrain from bidding more. Of course, for an advance sacrifice to succeed two conditions must be present. Firstly, the opponents need game (or slam) values and secondly they require a fit.

On this deal you can work out they must have the strength for game from LHO's strong artificial Two Club opening. You can deduce the existence of a fit for them from your strong diamond support. If your side possesses ten diamonds, there must be one suit in which you hold five cards or fewer. Much of the time your opponents will have a nine-card fit. If you jump to Five Diamonds, do you really believe North will pass or double? Even though he seems minimum for his initial action, he does hold seven solid spades that his partner cannot possibly know about. Surely, he will bid Five Spades. You easily beat this contract by overtaking the king of diamonds with the ace and laying down the king of clubs. Partner will show you an odd number of clubs and you will carry on with the suit. *Sacrificing can apply maximum pressure when done in advance*.

In our discussions, we have mentioned match-points and IMPs several times but have said little about other scoring methods. We would now like to redress the balance.

At rubber bridge, a bad time to sacrifice can come after you cut a weak partner. In this case, you do not wish to prolong the rubber and risk subsequent blunders from him. You must also take care if your opponents are poor declarers or poor bidders (and the inexperienced partnerships of the rubber bridge table create a greater than usual scope for misunderstanding). A sacrifice stands to gain the most if you have a score below the line that an opposing game or slam threatens to wipe out. In this case, you have more to lose if their contract makes.

It might appear that match-point pairs represents the best scoring method for sacrificing, but we beg to differ. If you misjudge and lose 800 against a vulnerable game or 500 against a non-vulnerable game, you will score a bottom. Even if you judge correctly and the sacrifice proves cheap, some pairs will have stopped in a part-score or overbid to a slam and you will hardly ever obtain a top. The best format for sacrificing is actually point-a-board (board-a-match). You expect teammates to reach any obvious games and to play the hand competently. If you misjudge, you cannot get a bottom; you just lose a board; however, if you are correct, you may win the board outright.

Golden Rule Seven:

Being Cautious in Save Situations can

. . . Protect you from going for a big number;
. . . Give you a chance of a plus score;
. . . Deter the enemy from finding a better spot;
. . . Avoid a near certain poor score.

Sacrificing can

. . . Work well when you expect it to be dirt cheap;
. . . Be very right if you might make your contract;
. . . Push your opposition a level higher;
. . . Apply maximum pressure when done in advance.

Rule Eight: Double Opposing Sacrifices

Take the money. This sounds like good advice and it often works. For sure, you do not want to let the opponents get away cheaply in an undoubled sacrifice. More to the point, you must be wary of allowing yourselves to be pushed. Having found the level at which you feel comfortable, you should stick to your guns and not allow the other side to convince you differently. If the penalty you gain comes close to the value of your own contract, you should score well enough.

East–West game
Dealer East

```
                        ♠ 8 7 3
                        ♡ Q 8 6 2
                        ◇ K Q 9 2
                        ♣ J 4

        ♠ K Q 6                      ♠ A J 10 9 4 2
        ♡ A K 10 5        N          ♡ 7 4
        ◇ 7 6          W     E       ◇ 3
        ♣ K 10 8 3        S          ♣ 9 6 5 2

                        ♠ 5
                        ♡ J 9 3
                        ◇ A J 10 8 5 4
                        ♣ A Q 7
```

YOU	LHO	PARTNER	RHO
–	–	2♠ *	3◇
4♠	5◇	Pass	Pass
?			

You would bid 4♠ on a wide range of hands – you might expect game to make easily or at least stand a chance, or it could be an advance sacrifice. This means partner has to pass when North advances to Five Diamonds and it is up to you to make the decision at the 5-level.

With your actual hand, you expected the spade game to make, but you cannot be at all sure of eleven tricks. You have solid defensive values and to score close to 620 you must double. As the cards lie, you can take two hearts, a heart ruff, a spade and a club: plus 500. ***Doubling opposing sacrifices can protect your score.***

Love All
Dealer West

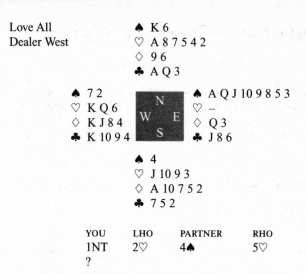

	♠ K 6	
	♡ A 8 7 5 4 2	
	◇ 9 6	
	♣ A Q 3	

♠ 7 2   ♠ A Q J 10 9 8 5 3
♡ K Q 6   ♡ –
◇ K J 8 4   ◇ Q 3
♣ K 10 9 4   ♣ J 8 6

♠ 4
♡ J 10 9 3
◇ A 10 7 5 2
♣ 7 5 2

YOU	LHO	PARTNER	RHO
1NT	2♡	4♠	5♡
?			

After describing your hand accurately with the weak 1NT opening, you may feel inclined to pass at this juncture. Indeed, having made a limit bid, you normally should aim to leave any further decisions to partner. However, you must consider his possible actions if you do pass. If he gambled Four Spades, perhaps intending it as much as an advance sacrifice as anything else, he will obviously pass out Five Hearts, happy to have pushed the opponents up to the five-level. By contrast, if he thought his contract would make, he will take some further action. You can guess from the opposing bidding and your heart holding that he probably holds a void in hearts. Such action will therefore take the form of a Five Spade bid. Is this really what you want to hear?

With no aces and the worst possible spade holding to put down in dummy, you hardly expect partner to make eleven tricks with spades as trumps. Fortunately, you can avoid this scenario by doubling Five Hearts. You have a sure trump trick (two if RHO turns up with the ♡A) and possible winners in each minor. Moreover, your relative shortage in spades increases the odds that partner's probable ace in the suit will stand up. As it happens, if he leads either minor, you will easily collect a reasonable 300 penalty against Five Hearts doubled. **_Doubling opposing sacrifices can stop from partner bidding on_**.

East–West game
Dealer West

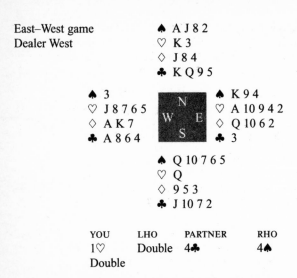

```
                  ♠ A J 8 2
                  ♡ K 3
                  ◇ J 8 4
                  ♣ K Q 9 5
♠ 3                              ♠ K 9 4
♡ J 8 7 6 5        N             ♡ A 10 9 4 2
◇ A K 7       W         E        ◇ Q 10 6 2
♣ A 8 6 4          S             ♣ 3
                  ♠ Q 10 7 6 5
                  ♡ Q
                  ◇ 9 5 3
                  ♣ J 10 7 2
```

YOU	LHO	PARTNER	RHO
1♡	Double	4♣	4♠
Double			

In this auction partner's double jump to Four Clubs retains its usual meaning as a Splinter, showing a decent raise to Four Hearts with either a singleton or void in clubs. (Some people play that after intervention both Three Clubs and Four Clubs are fit-showing jumps. However, you can describe a hand worth a raise to game with a source of tricks in clubs by making a three-level fit-jump and then bidding again, albeit with less of a pre-emptive effect.) In the current scenario, you know quite a lot about partner's hand; as well as the club shortage, you can feel quietly confident about finding him with a spade fragment, otherwise he might have preferred to go for a fit-showing jump of Three Diamonds.

You might venture Five Hearts, which will surely make if you find partner with decent trumps, ideally five. Indeed, the way the cards lie, North needs to cash the ace of spades to stop twelve tricks. All the same, surely you would rather give yourself the chance to pick up a massive penalty. You can almost count the first six tricks against Four Spades doubled: ace of clubs, club ruff, top diamond, club ruff, top diamond, club ruff (or overruff). This assumes next to no values in partner's hand. In practice his heart ace and diamond queen both represent defensive tricks and you collect 1100. ***Doubling opposing sacrifices can allow you to collect the occasional gift***.

East–West game
Dealer West

♠ K 6
♡ J 5
◇ Q 9 6 2
♣ A K J 9 5

♠ A J
♡ A 8 7 6 4 2
◇ A 10 3
♣ Q 4

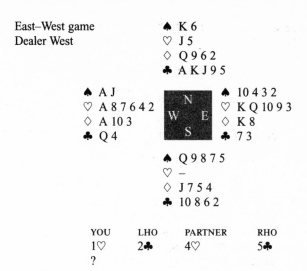

♠ 10 4 3 2
♡ K Q 10 9 3
◇ K 8
♣ 7 3

♠ Q 9 8 7 5
♡ –
◇ J 7 5 4
♣ 10 8 6 2

YOU	LHO	PARTNER	RHO
1♡	2♣	4♡	5♣
?			

Vulnerable against not, you know partner's pre-emptive raise to Four Hearts must contain some values and you were looking forward to playing the hand. Sadly, RHO's Five Club bid throws a spanner in the works. On this occasion, you must face the decision on your own – after a pre-emptive raise, a pass from you would not be forcing, and partner is unlikely to bid again, particularly if you think before passing. In our view, you are not very close to a Five Heart bid. This West hand screams 'Defend': You have no secondary heart values, no singleton and no outside source of tricks; furthermore, ♣Q-x is very likely useless offensively. True, partner might have a singleton club, but you know he will be too weak for a 4♣ Splinter.

Although even a handful of top players would consider passing, you do have three aces. In addition, partner might produce a trick of his own, and any values he has in the pointed suits could turn your ◇10 or ♠J into big cards. This gives you some insurance against the risk of an opposing heart void whilst opening up the possibility of a two-trick set. Remember that a double need not end the auction. Partner knows from their bidding that you do not hold a club stack and he can go on with the right hand. As the cards lie, you figure to pick up 300 if you find the diamond ruff and 100 otherwise; Five Hearts has no play and bidding it would give you a minus score. *Doubling opposing sacrifices can save you from going minus*.

```
         ♠ J                    ♠ A 4 2
         ♡ Q 9 6 5              ♡ A K J 8 4 3
         ◇ A K 9 6 4 3         ◇ 8 5
         ♣ J 2                  ♣ 9 7
```

YOU	LHO	PARTNER	RHO
–	–	1♡	2♡ *
4◇	Pass	4♡	4♠
?			

Your single jump to 4◇ shows length in the suit, support for hearts and is flexible on strength. Facing the hand illustrated, you want to go on to the almost laydown 5♡ rather than defend RHO's black two-suiter for at best a one-trick set. So, should you bid 5♡?

Well, on another day partner might turn up with this hand:

```
              ♠ K 10 5
              ♡ A 10 8 7 4
              ◇ 5
              ♣ K Q 8 4
```

Now you want to defend Four Spades doubled. You cannot tell which hand partner has, but you must tell him that you expected 4♡ to make. To do this, you double 4♠. This is not a penalty double – it simply says that you have some high cards. Now partner will make the right decision, usually based on his diamond fit and strength in spades. *Doubling opposing sacrifices can say this is our hand*.

```
         ♠ A K Q 9 4 2        ♠ J 8 6 5
         ♡ 10 4                ♡ 6
         ◇ K 3                 ◇ A 10 7 4
         ♣ Q J 5               ♣ A K 8 3
```

YOU	LHO	PARTNER	RHO
1♠	2♡	4♡ *	5♡
?			

The opposing bidding has removed the space for a cue bid or RKCB. If you simply bid 5♠, partner will not read it as a slam try. He will think you are just competing.

To convey your slam ambitions you should pass, clearly forcing in this instance, and, if partner doubles, bid Five Spades next round. This must mean something different from a direct 5♠ and is widely played as expressing interest in a slam. ***Do not double opposing sacrifices if passing and then bidding can show slam interest.***

East–West game
Dealer East

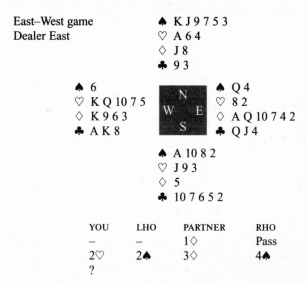

	♠ K J 9 7 5 3	
	♡ A 6 4	
	◇ J 8	
	♣ 9 3	
♠ 6		♠ Q 4
♡ K Q 10 7 5		♡ 8 2
◇ K 9 6 3		◇ A Q 10 7 4 2
♣ A K 8		♣ Q J 4
	♠ A 10 8 2	
	♡ J 9 3	
	◇ 5	
	♣ 10 7 6 5 2	

YOU	LHO	PARTNER	RHO
–	–	1◇	Pass
2♡	2♠	3◇	4♠
?			

When you chose to jump shift, you did so on the strength of the diamond support. Obviously, you do want not to defend below the level of game in the suit, particularly never having shown support. Having already created a game force, you could pass, but partner will remain in doubt as to whether you have good hearts or a diamond fit. Whenever you get the chance to resolve an ambiguity, you should take it: call 5◇. This is not a shut-out bid. If partner has extra values and at least one major-suit ace, he can press on to a slam. ***Do not double opposing sacrifices if you are confident of better things.***

You will notice that on the last two sequences (and the one on page 88), the bidding revealed to both of you that the partnership held game values. This allowed the option of a forcing pass. Other situations in which people would normally play a pass as forcing can include when the opponents try to stop in a part-score and only bid game after you do, and when they overcall your strong 2♣ opening.

East–West game
Dealer East

	♠	—
	♡	A 8 7
	◇	A Q 9 8 5 2
	♣	J 10 9 6

♠ A Q 9 7 6 4 3   ♠ K J 2
♡ K J 2   ♡ Q 10 3
◇ 6   ◇ 7 3
♣ K 4   ♣ A Q 8 5 3

♠ 10 8 5
♡ 9 6 5 4
◇ K J 10 4
♣ 7 2

YOU	LHO	PARTNER	RHO
–	–	1♣	Pass
1♠	2◇	2♠	3◇
4◇ *	5◇	Pass	Pass
?			

It looks as if only the broken spade suit deterred you from starting with a jump shift and you were certainly worth the Four Diamond cue bid once partner raised your suit. (Presumably you are not playing support doubles, as then he would have four-card spade support). Here the fact you have made a slam try makes this unequivocally 'your hand' and hence partner's pass is forcing.

He has judged well because although he has no extra values, he knows that holding nothing in diamonds will fit well with your hand. His failure to double tells you that he is happy to hear you bid again and that he cannot envisage collecting a huge penalty from Five Diamonds doubled. Given this information, it is automatic to go on. By no stretch of the imagination have you promised a seven-card suit. Knowing that partner does not particularly wish to defend, neither do you. It probably costs nothing to try a Five Heart cue bid, but he will now sign off in Five Spades. ***Do not double opposing sacrifices if you hold unexpected length in your suit.***

For our final example, we continue with the forcing pass theme. If you have already bid to a small slam, you should only invite a grand slam with first-round control in the enemy suit. Moreover, if 7NT is the main option left in the picture, the control must be the ace.

```
♠ Q 4              ♠ A K 10 7 6
♡ K Q 7            ♡ A J 8
◇ –                ◇ 9
♣ K Q J 9 7 5 4 3  ♣ A 10 8 2
```

Love All: Dealer East

YOU	LHO	PARTNER	RHO
–	–	1♠	Pass
3♣	5◇	6♣	6◇
?			

Partner has no reason to believe that you hold a hand suitable for 6♠ or 6NT, so a pass from you would promise first-round diamond control and invite him to try Seven Clubs. On this deal, this is exactly what you want. Whilst you like the hand very much, with no aces you cannot bid seven on your own. If he turns up with nothing wasted in diamonds, you are effectively playing with a 30-point deck, and you should have enough for a grand slam. With his hand as shown, he clearly will bid 7♣. However, if RHO then sacrifices in 7◇, you will have to double. A pass from you would show the ◇A and invite partner to bid 7NT. *Do not double opposing sacrifices if you want to invite a grand slam with a first-round control.*

Golden Rule Eight:

Doubling Opposing Sacrifices can

. . . Protect your score;
. . . Stop partner from bidding on;
. . . Allow you to collect the occasional gift;
. . . Save you from going minus;
. . . Say this is our hand.

Do not Double Opposing Sacrifices if

. . . Passing and then bidding can show slam interest;
. . . You are confident of better things;
. . . You hold unexpected length in your suit;
. . . You want to invite a grand slam with a first-round control.

Rule Nine: When in Doubt Bid One More

In the previous two chapters, we considered what to do if it was clear who owned the hand. We now turn to the scenario when you cannot readily tell who can make what. Here the general rule is 'When in doubt bid one more'. A simple rationale lies behind this advice. If you exchange plus fifty or a hundred for a small minus, you lose little (except perhaps at pairs). By contrast, if at least one contract makes, you want to be declaring. Figures such as 790, 620 and 550 you always want in the home column – slam scores even more so.

Please note that this rule does not provide an excuse for you to overbid. We cannot stress too strongly the need to attach as much weight to the words 'When in doubt' as to the others.

Love All
Dealer South

♠	K 9 6 5		
♡	K J 4		
◇	Q 10 3 2		
♣	Q 5		

♠ 7	♠ A J 8 4 3
♡ 6	♡ 10 5
◇ A K 9 4	◇ 7 5
♣ A J 10 8 7 6 4	♣ K 9 3 2

♠ Q 10 2
♡ A Q 9 8 7 3 2
◇ J 8 6
♣ —

YOU	LHO	PARTNER	RHO
–	–	–	3♡
4♣	4♡	5♣	5♡
?			

The opposing bidding means this deal involves some guesswork, but some things you can be sure about. Knowing partner likes your clubs, there is a good chance the suit will play for no loser, and if he can contribute an ace, you may well make a slam. Bid 6♣. *Bidding one more when in doubt can put you in a making contract*.

Love All
Dealer North

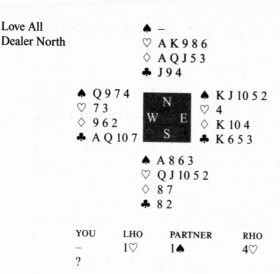

```
                        ♠ —
                        ♡ A K 9 8 6
                        ♢ A Q J 5 3
                        ♣ J 9 4
     ♠ Q 9 7 4                        ♠ K J 10 5 2
     ♡ 7 3            N               ♡ 4
     ♢ 9 6 2       W     E            ♢ K 10 4
     ♣ A Q 10 7       S               ♣ K 6 5 3
                        ♠ A 8 6 3
                        ♡ Q J 10 5 2
                        ♢ 8 7
                        ♣ 8 2
```

YOU	LHO	PARTNER	RHO
–	1♡	1♠	4♡
?			

In an uncontested response to the overcall, you would hardly dream of going all the way to Four Spades. Still, we can see several reasons for taking the plunge now the auction has gone the way it has. For a start, their game might make: you possess only one sure defensive trick and a non-vulnerable one-level overcall will often contain fewer than three. For another, your spade game could be on, particularly if the hands fit well; whilst opener could turn up with extras, RHO's hand is generally limited by the fact that he probably had stronger ways available to show a heart raise. True, partner would have another bid if you passed smoothly (and you would get a bit of time to do so if, as in duplicate bridge, RHO says 'Stop' or pulls out a 'Stop' card before bidding Four Hearts), but he might hold an unsuitable hand for making a flexible re-opening double. Finally, and this proves the point on this example, if you bid 4♠, you give the opponents the chance to call 5♡ and go one down. Sure enough, with two powerful 5-card suits and a void in spades, LHO can lay claim to considerable reserves of playing strength and will feel fully justified in advancing to Five Hearts. In all probability therefore, your Four Spade bid will transform –420 into +50, and if they decide to defend, you only go one down – a great save against 4♡. *Bidding one more when in doubt can push the opponents higher*.

East–West game
Dealer West

♠ K J 7
♡ K 5 2
◇ 5 3
♣ A K 10 5 4

♠ Q 8 6 3
♡ Q J 10
◇ A K 10 9 6 4
♣ —

♠ 10 4
♡ A 8 4
◇ Q J 8 7 2
♣ J 9 3

♠ A 9 5 2
♡ 9 7 6 3
◇ —
♣ Q 8 7 6 2

YOU	LHO	PARTNER	RHO
1◇	2♣	3◇	5♣
?			

Vulnerable against not, partner's jump raise must show some values as well as some diamond length. If you catch him with both major-suit kings, or the ace-jack of spades over the king, or the ace of hearts over the king, you will probably manage eleven tricks with diamonds as trumps. This serves as an important consideration at this vulnerability because you should only bid a contract if you see some hope of making it. Added to this, your defensive prospects seem poor. One of your two top diamonds might stand up, but then you are scratching around for tricks. If partner had the option to make a cue bid to indicate a value raise, you can rest assured that he has few defensive tricks up his sleeve.

As the cards lie you make Five Diamonds when the heart finesse works and, for the same reason, their Five Clubs would go one down. The opponents do best to sacrifice in Six Clubs, but they may find this quite hard to judge. LHO holds as flat a hand as is possible on the auction (indeed some people would prefer a take-out double to the 2♣ overcall) and RHO surely shot his bolt with 5♣.

Now consider what would happen if we swapped the king and nine of hearts. The heart finesse no longer works for you in 5◇, but it does for them in 5♣. If they double, −200 still represents a cheap save against the opposing club game. ***Bidding one more when in doubt can give you a two-way bet.***

Game All
Dealer North

```
                    ♠ A 4
                    ♡ K Q 7 5 4 3
                    ◇ A 7 4 3
                    ♣ 5
    ♠ K Q 7 6              ♠ J 10 3
    ♡ 10 8 6       N       ♡ –
    ◇ 8 2       W     E    ◇ K J 9 5
    ♣ Q 10 6 3     S       ♣ A K J 9 8 7
                    ♠ 9 8 5 2
                    ♡ A J 9 2
                    ◇ Q 10 6
                    ♣ 4 2
```

YOU	LHO	PARTNER	RHO
–	1♡	2♣	2♡
3♣	3◇	4♣	4♡
?			

Perhaps you would prefer a pre-emptive jump to Four Clubs at your first turn, but the simple raise seems reasonable: sometimes it can prove a mistake to announce strong support for partner when you expect to be outbid. You now need to reassess the situation in the light of the subsequent bidding.

At first glance, it seems as if they may have stretched. LHO made a game try and, although RHO appears to have accepted this, he may feel none too confident of making Four Hearts, bidding it either to induce a phantom sacrifice or simply to avoid having to defend. Even so, your two smallish diamonds trigger warning flashes – the opponents may own a two-suit fit in the reds. In these situations, you should, as usual, attach more weight to partner's actions than to those of your opponents. If he wants to defend Four Hearts, he might make a stronger bid over Three Diamonds than Four Clubs, such as a cue bid of Three Hearts. Alternatively, he could lie in wait. The way he has bid indicates a preparedness for you to bid Five Clubs with a suitable hand. This you surely possess. Indeed their Four Hearts is cold and Five Clubs depends on the diamond guess, one partner figures to get right on the bidding, especially if, as seems probable, RHO leads the ♡A at trick one. *Bidding one more when in doubt can prevent the loss of a double game swing*.

Love All
Dealer South

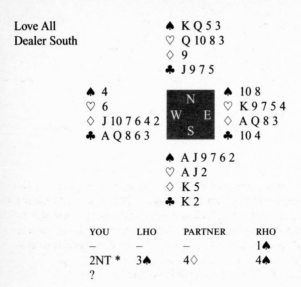

	♠ K Q 5 3
	♡ Q 10 8 3
	◇ 9
	♣ J 9 7 5

♠ 4   ♠ 10 8
♡ 6   ♡ K 9 7 5 4
◇ J 10 7 6 4 2   ◇ A Q 8 3
♣ A Q 8 6 3   ♣ 10 4

     ♠ A J 9 7 6 2
     ♡ A J 2
     ◇ K 5
     ♣ K 2

YOU	LHO	PARTNER	RHO
–	–	–	1♠
2NT *	3♠	4◇	4♠
?			

This auction resembles the previous one in several ways. You establish a fit in one the minors, bid up to the four level in it, and hear the opponents contract for game in their major. This time, you have taken up more of their bidding room, leaving them no scope for a game try. This should make you a bit more wary of taking an action whose success depends on the outcome of their contract. That said, RHO, if he is sensible, would take account of the likelihood of bad breaks and the consequentially increased danger of a double. Furthermore, the fact that partner has expressed preference for the longer of your two suits means you should possess a decent fit, most likely one of ten cards. This should both safeguard you against the possibility of conceding a hefty penalty and reduce the defensive potential of whatever diamond values partner holds. If we have failed to convince you of the case for bidding Five Diamonds, this is almost intentional. You can thus decide what to do on the basis of the rule. In a genuine case of doubt, you should bid one more.

Five Diamonds has play, needing two finesses and reasonable breaks, but in practice goes one down. This still represents a good save against Four Spades. If they push on to five, they too would be one off when, as expected, the ♡K sits onside but the ♣A does not. ***Bidding one more when in doubt can effect a cheap sacrifice.***

♠ A Q 10 9 8 4 2   ♠ K J
♡ –   ♡ 9 8 7 4
♢ K 10 8 3   ♢ A Q J 9 4
♣ 8 7   ♣ J 2

Game All: Dealer North

YOU	LHO	PARTNER	RHO
–	Pass	1♢	2NT (Unusual)
4♠	5♡	5♠	6♡
?			

On this deal, everything in the play may depend on the first trick. In Six Spades, any lead bar a club will probably allow you to take twelve tricks. If the opposing hands look something like yours – and RHO's decision to bid again suggests he has a void somewhere – the wrong choice of lead could let through Six Hearts. Let them make the mistake. Bid Six Spades.

This was the full deal in an International match:

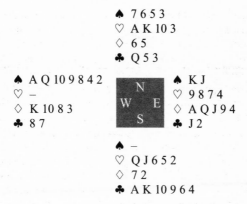

♠ 7 6 5 3
♡ A K 10 3
♢ 6 5
♣ Q 5 3

♠ A Q 10 9 8 4 2   ♠ K J
♡ –   ♡ 9 8 7 4
♢ K 10 8 3   ♢ A Q J 9 4
♣ 8 7   ♣ J 2

♠ –
♡ Q J 6 5 2
♢ 7 2
♣ A K 10 9 6 4

The Irish West advanced to Six Spades and was richly rewarded when everyone passed and North elected to lead a top heart. The auction started the same way at the other table, but West passed over Six Hearts and East decided to double and lead the king of spades. Ireland thus recorded a slam at both tables and earned a huge swing on the board. ***Bidding one more when in doubt can transfer an opening lead guess to the opponents***.

♠ 10 5 4	YOU	LHO	PARTNER	RHO
♡ K 6 3	–	–	2♡ *	2♠
◇ K J 10	?			
♣ Q 9 8 3				

Non-vulnerable we see a good case for raising to 3♡. For one thing, if LHO becomes declarer, presumably in a no-trump contract, you are happy to see partner lead a heart. For another, it removes a whole round of bidding from LHO. You exclude the option of a 2NT call and, if he bids 3♠, his partner cannot readily tell whether this invites game. True, some pairs play that a double of 3♡ serves as a game try, leaving 3♠ available as a competitive move, but in this case, you could leave him fixed on a good hand lacking primary spade support. You hardly need worry that partner will continue to game. You would make a stronger move, using a 2NT relay perhaps, if your interest extended beyond the part-score level. ***Bidding one more when in doubt can remove their space for making a game try***.

♠ A Q J 6 3 2	YOU	LHO	PARTNER	RHO
♡ 7 4	2♠ *	Pass	3♠	4♡
◇ 10 6 5	?			
♣ Q 3				

Your Weak Two described your hand well, which puts partner in a much better position than you to judge what to do over Four Hearts. Some people go so far as to say that a pre-emptor should never bid again. We regard that view as extreme, but you would still need a strong reason to act in front of partner – a void heart, maybe. Whilst normally you would hope partner produces three-card support for his raise (on the basis that the three level is normally safe with nine trumps), he never guarantees it. If he wants to play in game facing a maximum, he would enquire about your range with 2NT. His raise merely indicates a desire to make life as difficult as possible for your RHO. Partner may possess enough to double Four Hearts, or at any rate to defeat it, or he may have so little that you would concede a sizeable penalty in Four Spades doubled. You should not try to bid his hand. Just bid yours – pass. ***Do not bid one more when in doubt if you have already shown your full hand***.

Game All   ♠ A 7 3
Dealer East   ♡ A J 8 7 4
                        ◇ J 2
                        ♣ Q 5 3

♠ K Q   ♠ J 9 4
♡ 6 3   ♡ 10
◇ A K 8 7 6 4   ◇ Q 10 5 3
♣ 10 9 4   ♣ A K 7 6 2

                  ♠ 10 8 6 5 2
                  ♡ K Q 9 5 2
                  ◇ 9
                  ♣ J 8

YOU	LHO	PARTNER	RHO
–	–	Pass	Pass
1◇	1♡	3♣	4♡
?			

Sometimes, when continually faced with problems of your own, you can forget that bridge is a partnership game. Everyone says that sharing a problem can halve it, and the same can apply at the bridge table. On occasion, you do need to take a unilateral decision, but if you are in doubt and you believe that partner will be in at least a good position to judge, you should try to consult him.

On a hand like West's, one can get carried away by what sounds like a two-suit fit (partner's jump shift as a passed hand obviously showing both diamond support and a club suit). Indeed at the table the International player holding these cards elected to bid 4NT, offering his partner a choice of games. Unfortunately, with a club, a heart and a spade to lose, he could not make a winning choice. Worse still, Four Hearts would go two off if the defenders manage to untangle their spades, and one off otherwise.

You do much better to pass the decision to partner. He can infer from your failure either to double Four Hearts or to drive the bidding to the five level that on a defensive versus offensive scale your hand lies somewhere in the middle. Holding barely any more shape than he has already shown, he will defend. ***Do not bid one more when in doubt if partner should be involved in the decision.***

Love All   ♠ J 8 5
Dealer West   ♡ –
                  ◇ A Q J 7 5 3
                  ♣ Q 10 6 5

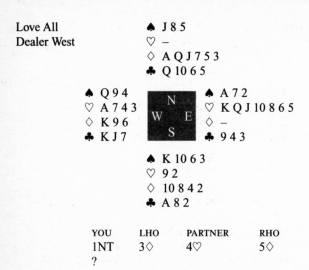

     ♠ Q 9 4   ♠ A 7 2
     ♡ A 7 4 3   ♡ K Q J 10 8 6 5
     ◇ K 9 6   ◇ –
     ♣ K J 7   ♣ 9 4 3

               ♠ K 10 6 3
               ♡ 9 2
               ◇ 10 8 4 2
               ♣ A 8 2

YOU	LHO	PARTNER	RHO
1NT	3◇	4♡	5◇
?			

In this auction partner has gone Four Hearts facing what might be a doubleton. You actually possess four-card support, considerably better than minimum. It would appear that your heart length would both cover any holes in partner's suit if he plays the hand and reduce his defensive potential. In practice, your four hearts may matter less than this assessment suggests. He will surely hold a decent six- or seven-card suit, and whether you turn up with A-x or A-x-x-x may make little difference to what heart tricks he makes. Once you cast doubt on the usefulness of your main offensive feature, the attraction of bidding Five Hearts loses its gloss. The other characteristics of your hand all point in the other direction: you have no obvious ruffing potential, your values in the black suits may come in just as handy with diamonds as trumps, and your diamond holding is principally defensive. Facing either a singleton or void ◇K-x-x may contribute little in a heart contract, particularly with the lead going through it at trick one. There is no need to double Five Diamonds to tell partner what sort of hand you hold. Your 12-14 1NT opening bid did that. It seems a close call, but we suspect most experts would vote for a pass – very likely the winning move if partner bid Four Hearts on a wing and a prayer. ***Do not bid one more when in doubt if your values in their suit are wasted facing a shortage.***

East–West game
Dealer East

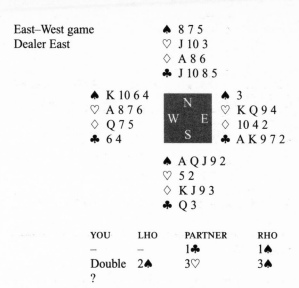

	♠ 8 7 5	
	♡ J 10 3	
	◇ A 8 6	
	♣ J 10 8 5	

♠ K 10 6 4		♠ 3
♡ A 8 7 6	N	♡ K Q 9 4
◇ Q 7 5	W E	◇ 10 4 2
♣ 6 4	S	♣ A K 9 7 2

	♠ A Q J 9 2	
	♡ 5 2	
	◇ K J 9 3	
	♣ Q 3	

YOU	LHO	PARTNER	RHO
–	–	1♣	1♠
Double	2♠	3♡	3♠
?			

On the first round, some people would bid a number of no-trumps to indicate the stopper in spades, but we agree with the negative double. By telling partner about the four-card heart suit, you retain the option to bid no-trumps later; it works less well the other way round. Indeed the auction has suited this strategy neatly. You have unearthed a heart fit whilst keeping the opponents in the dark about your strong spades. Ordinarily one strains to bid vulnerable games at IMPs or at rubber, but one must temper optimism with realism. In this case, partner may have already stretched to avoid being shut out over LHO's raise to Two Spades. Once you downgrade your king of spades facing a known singleton (or possibly a void), you really have nothing to justify pressing on. Now regarding this as a competitive part-score deal, the winning action becomes apparent. You possess an eight-card heart fit and they have eight spades, which suggests a total of 16 tricks. This implies that if Four Hearts were on, Three Spades would go three down. If you can double for penalties, do so. If not (because a second double would simply promise extra values and invite partner to express his opinion), you will have to grit your teeth and pass. *Do not bid one more when in doubt if a count of total tricks says neither contract is on.*

♠ A 9 7		♠ K Q 10 8 6 2	
♡ J 5		♡ 7 4	
◇ K J 6 3		◇ Q 8	
♣ J 10 9 7		♣ 6 4 2	

YOU	LHO	PARTNER	RHO
–	–	2♠ *	3♡
?			

In view of what we said on page 100, you will appreciate that a raise of the Weak Two to Three Spades would prove totally fatuous. It does not invite partner to save or to bid game for other reasons. Much more likely, you will simply push your opponents into game – LHO might call 4♡ just because he does not wish to defend, and you give RHO a second chance to bid. If you are going to bid on this collection, and at the right vulnerability you would, you must jump to Four Spades. Let them guess your intentions. ***Do not bid one more when in doubt if you want to avoid pushing them into game.***

Golden Rule Nine:

Bidding One More when in Doubt can

. . . Put you in a making contract;
. . . Push the opponents higher;
. . . Give you a two-way bet;
. . . Prevent the loss of a double game swing;
. . . Effect a cheap sacrifice;
. . . Transfer an opening lead guess to the opponents;
. . . Remove their space for making a game try.

Do not Bid One More when in Doubt if

. . . You have already shown your full hand;
. . . Partner should be involved in the decision;
. . . Your values in their suit are wasted facing a shortage;
. . . A count of total trumps says neither contract is on;
. . . You want to avoid pushing them into game.

Rule Ten: Leave the Five Level to the Enemy

How many times have you heard someone say 'It is easier to take three tricks than eleven'? If you have played for a while, we bet quite a few. We are happy to confirm that, except on really freakish deals, the statement does indeed hold true. Yes, in some ways this rule resembles rule 8, which dealt with opposing sacrifices, but rule 10 applies whether they own the hand, nobody does, or you cannot tell.

Apart from the obvious desire to avoid turning a plus into a minus, you will come across other motivations to sell out at the five level, as we see in our first example:

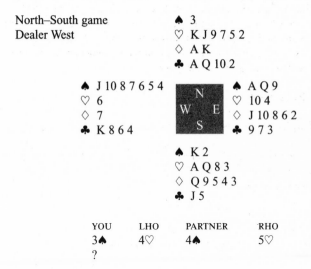

North–South game
Dealer West

♠ 3
♡ K J 9 7 5 2
♢ A K
♣ A Q 10 2

♠ J 10 8 7 6 5 4
♡ 6
♢ 7
♣ K 8 6 4

♠ A Q 9
♡ 10 4
♢ J 10 8 6 2
♣ 9 7 3

♠ K 2
♡ A Q 8 3
♢ Q 9 5 4 3
♣ J 5

YOU	LHO	PARTNER	RHO
3♠	4♡	4♠	5♡
?			

As a rule, you should rarely bid again after making a pre-emptive bid. Partner knows what is going on better than you do. This time you hold two singletons, but this still provides insufficient excuse to take charge. If partner bid 4♠ as a save, your opponents may belong in a slam and you not want to do to push them into it. Okay, you might then bid 6♠, but this could be a phantom. *Leaving the five level to the enemy can spare you the need to face a slam-level decision*.

Even if you exclude slam bidding from the equation, one situation in which it almost always proves right to leave the five level to the enemy occurs when your side's sacrifice pushes them from four to five of a major. If the field, or the other room, as the case may be, has been allowed to play at the four level, you will either tie (if at least eleven tricks make) or win if they go one down. If instead the normal result would come from a double by them, repeating the sacrifice very likely means you concede an extra 200 or 300 and normally guarantees you a losing board.

North–South game
Dealer South

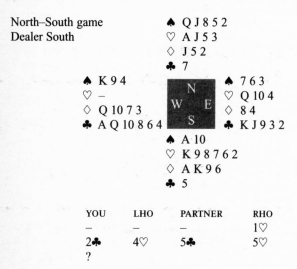

```
                    ♠ Q J 8 5 2
                    ♡ A J 5 3
                    ◇ J 5 2
                    ♣ 7
   ♠ K 9 4                        ♠ 7 6 3
   ♡ –                            ♡ Q 10 4
   ◇ Q 10 7 3                     ◇ 8 4
   ♣ A Q 10 8 6 4                 ♣ K J 9 3 2
                    ♠ A 10
                    ♡ K 9 8 7 6 2
                    ◇ A K 9 6
                    ♣ 5
```

YOU	LHO	PARTNER	RHO
–	–	–	1♡
2♣	4♡	5♣	5♡
?			

Looking at the West hand, you cannot say for sure who owns the hand. However, the vulnerability increases the likelihood that partner bid Five Clubs because he thought Four Hearts would make and the fact that your vulnerable RHO has gone on to Five Hearts suggests he senses a chance of making eleven tricks. If you push on to Six Clubs, you throw away all the advantage of having pushed your opponents to the five level as then you are sure to go minus. Five Hearts looks a good contract, but with trumps 3-0 offside and the spade finesse wrong, declarer ends up one down. *Leaving the five level to the enemy can enable you to cash in your advantage*.

We have mentioned the law of total tricks several times already, and we hope you are familiar with it by now. The law implies that for both sides to take eleven tricks, the total trick count would need to come to 22. This happens very rarely. Of course, you will normally want to bid on over their five level bid if there are 21 total trumps, as one contract or the other figures to make. If there are only 19 or 20 total trumps, and deals containing 19 or 20 trumps come up far more often than those with 21 or 22, you will generally want to defend.

Love All
Dealer East

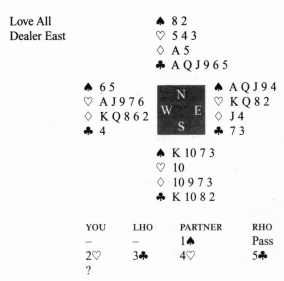

```
                    ♠ 8 2
                    ♡ 5 4 3
                    ◇ A 5
                    ♣ A Q J 9 6 5
     ♠ 6 5                        ♠ A Q J 9 4
     ♡ A J 9 7 6         N        ♡ K Q 8 2
     ◇ K Q 8 6 2      W     E     ◇ J 4
     ♣ 4                 S        ♣ 7 3
                    ♠ K 10 7 3
                    ♡ 10
                    ◇ 10 9 7 3
                    ♣ K 10 8 2
```

YOU	LHO	PARTNER	RHO
–	–	1♠	Pass
2♡	3♣	4♡	5♣
?			

Your Two Heart response promised five hearts, so you hold no extra length in the suit. Whilst your source of tricks in diamonds gives you a reason maybe to contemplate bidding one for the road, it is not enough. You should see little reason to put partner with a diamond fit, and you can offer scant support for his spades. With two probable defensive tricks facing a partner who can both open and bid again, you would expect to defeat Five Clubs by two tricks and feel sure of beating it by at least one. To throw away such a seemingly certain penalty, you would need to feel supremely confident of taking eleven tricks. With this hand, you cannot do so. ***Leaving the five level to the enemy can let you try for three tricks instead of eleven.***

When you own a more offensively orientated hand than you have shown, it can seem tempting to tell partner this by making a further bid. However, you should resist the temptation to make a unilateral decision unless you hold many extras. When both sides bid to a high level, a shortage in their suit (other than a void) loses its worth. If you both possess a singleton in their suit, neither of you has a ruffing value. A doubleton in the short trump hand will hardly ever yield a ruffing trick – partner will invariably be as short or shorter than you.

Love All
Dealer South

♠ 7 5 2
♥ J 6
♦ 8 7 5 2
♣ A K 9 6

♠ A Q J 6   ♠ K 10 8 3
♥ Q 9 4   ♥ K 7 5 2
♦ K J 10 4   ♦ A Q 9 6
♣ 7 4   ♣ 3

♠ 9 4
♥ A 10 8 3
♦ 3
♣ Q J 10 8 5 2

YOU	LHO	PARTNER	RHO
–	–	–	Pass
1NT	Pass	2♣ *	Double
2♠	3♣	4♠	5♣
?			

In several ways, we like the texture of this hand. Although only mid-range for a 12-14 1NT, your spades look excellent and you have nothing wasted in clubs. In addition, your chunky diamonds could provide a source of tricks. Even so, you must refrain from bidding 5♠. Partner's Stayman bid suggests he may well turn up with only four spades. At this level, possession of merely an eight-card fit gives reason alone to defend. Furthermore, your doubleton club, which initially appeared useful, has lost all its potential as a ruffing value with the opponents' big club fit coming to light. You should pass and leave the decision to partner, who will double. ***Leaving the five level to the enemy can involve partner in the decision***.

You are most likely to bid on over their five-level contract when your side alone is vulnerable. Let us suppose that you expect to defeat the enemy contract by two tricks and you do not expect them to double your contract. If you can pick up 650 instead of 300, you can gain 350, almost as much as you stand to lose if you concede 100 instead of scooping 300. At equal vulnerability, as in the last example, the difference between 300 and 450 or 500 and 650 comes to just 150. When you add in the fact that if you are confident of a two trick set, a chance must exist of three-trick defeat, you will nearly always want to take the money at rubber or teams scoring.

East–West game
Dealer North

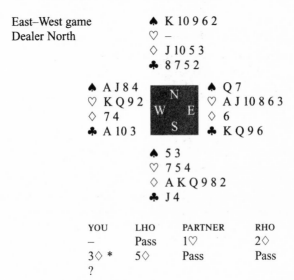

	♠ K 10 9 6 2
	♡ –
	◇ J 10 5 3
	♣ 8 7 5 2

♠ A J 8 4	♠ Q 7
♡ K Q 9 2	♡ A J 10 8 6 3
◇ 7 4	◇ 6
♣ A 10 3	♣ K Q 9 6

	♠ 5 3
	♡ 7 5 4
	◇ A K Q 9 8 2
	♣ J 4

YOU	LHO	PARTNER	RHO
–	Pass	1♡	2◇
3◇ *	5◇	Pass	Pass
?			

Even assuming your value-showing raise on the first round was not a game force, it surely suffices to make partner's pass forcing, an invitation to go on. Certainly, if you could have passed a 3♡ rebid, you have plenty in reserve. Furthermore, depending upon whether partner's opening bid showed five hearts (in which case you might hold only three), your trump support is either better or much better than he might expect. Either way your king-queen will fill in the gaps in his suit but prove useless defending. You should therefore break the rule and bid 5♡. *Not leaving the five level to the enemy can be right when you really expect to make your contract.*

A few pages back we suggested that if you thought there were 20 or 21 total trumps you should bid five of your suit over five of theirs. Of course, in real life, nobody holds up a flag and says how many cards they hold in their long suit. Sometimes you have to make an educated guess. Whilst match-pointed pairs places an emphasis on plus scores, other scoring methods give more weight to big swings. If both sides are anywhere close to making, you should often take out insurance to protect against the possibility of a double game swing.

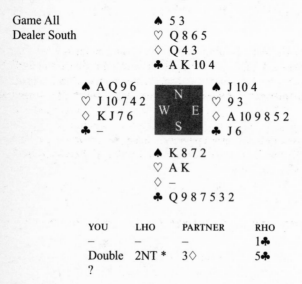

Game All
Dealer South

```
                    ♠ 5 3
                    ♡ Q 8 6 5
                    ◊ Q 4 3
                    ♣ A K 10 4

  ♠ A Q 9 6                        ♠ J 10 4
  ♡ J 10 7 4 2          N          ♡ 9 3
  ◊ K J 7 6        W        E       ◊ A 10 9 8 5 2
  ♣ -                   S           ♣ J 6

                    ♠ K 8 7 2
                    ♡ A K
                    ◊ -
                    ♣ Q 9 8 7 5 3 2
```

YOU	LHO	PARTNER	RHO
–	–	–	1♣
Double	2NT *	3◊	5♣
?			

On this auction, we assume RHO's One Club promised a club suit and LHO's 2NT showed a raise to at least Three Clubs. (Similar principles could apply if they use a prepared club – LHO would hold more clubs for his bid and RHO would need correspondingly fewer to go 5♣.) On the losing trick count, your hand is better than it might be: you have six rather than seven. Moreover, you possess four-card diamond support and a void in their suit. Partner may guess your hand contains one of these features but not both. Whilst you might worry about club values in his hand and be wary of taking a decision in front of him, you really have no choice. If Five Diamonds from you proves costly, his 3◊ was the mistake. ***Not leaving the five level to the enemy can save you from losing a double game swing.***

♠ –		♠ 10 6 3
♡ 6		♡ J 9 7 4 3
◊ K Q 10 7 6 4		◊ 3
♣ Q 10 8 7 5 3		♣ A K 9 2

North–South game: dealer South

YOU	LHO	PARTNER	RHO
–	–	–	1♠
2NT *	4♠	5♣	5♠
?			

Since your Unusual 2NT only promised ten cards in the minors, you hold two more cards than partner might expect. Your sixth card in each minor may mean the hand plays two tricks better than would a 5-5 hand with similar values. This suggests Five Clubs might have made or been only one down. Therefore, you reckon on losing 100 or maybe 300 in Six Clubs doubled. This gives you a sufficient margin to make up for those times when partner turns up with enough to beat Five Spades. *Not leaving the five level to the enemy can work well if you are confident a sacrifice is worthwhile*.

Golden Rule Ten:

Leaving the Five Level to the Enemy can

. . . Spare you the need to face a slam-level decision;
. . . Enable you to cash in your advantage;
. . . Let you try for three tricks instead of eleven;
. . . Involve partner in the decision.

Not Leaving the Five Level to the Enemy can

. . . Be right when you really expect to make your contract;
. . . Save you from losing a double game swing;
. . . Work well if you are confident a sacrifice is worthwhile.

Rule Eleven: Do Not Double Them into Game

Contracts from $2\heartsuit$ to $4\diamondsuit$ are part-scores undoubled but yield game if doubled and made. If there is one way to ensure nobody wants to cut you at the rubber bridge table, it is to acquire a reputation for doubling opponents into game. At pairs, one also needs to take care. All too often, people go in search of the magic 200 when in practice any plus on a part-score deal frequently scores quite well.

The odds tend to work against any marginal doubles. With IMP scoring and the opponents non-vulnerable you stand to gain 2 IMPs if you change +50 to +100 whilst you will lose 8 if –110 becomes –470. Even if they go two light, and you convert +100 into +300, that is only 5 IMPs. In general, you should only risk doubling them into game if you expect to beat their contract by two tricks. This gives you a margin for error.

♠ 8 6 4	YOU	LHO	PARTNER	RHO
♡ K 7 6 5 3	–	–	1♠	2♡
◇ 10 4 2	Pass	Pass	Double	Pass
♣ 8 3	?			

Such poor heart intermediates and three-card spade support make this decision painless. Bid Two Spades. Who knows, someone may compete to $3\heartsuit$. Then you can double having limited your hand and disclosed your spade support.

♠ Q 8 5 2	YOU	LHO	PARTNER	RHO
♡ 6 2	–	–	1NT	2♠
◇ K 10 7 4	?			
♣ Q 6 3				

For this example we assume you use a weak no-trump and play that a double of 2♠ would be penalty. (Many pairs play Lebensohl or a variant thereof, in which case a double would not mean penalties.) This time you expect Two Spades to fail more often than it makes, but you need better odds to double. Just pass. *Not doubling them into game can save you from needlessly conceding a game*.

Game All
Dealer South

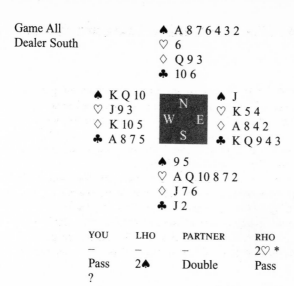

♠ A 8 7 6 4 3 2
♡ 6
♢ Q 9 3
♣ 10 6

♠ K Q 10
♡ J 9 3
♢ K 10 5
♣ A 8 7 5

♠ J
♡ K 5 4
♢ A 8 4 2
♣ K Q 9 4 3

♠ 9 5
♡ A Q 10 8 7 2
♢ J 7 6
♣ J 2

YOU	LHO	PARTNER	RHO
–	–	–	2♡ *
Pass	2♠	Double	Pass
?			

If you defend when you believe your side can make game, you may find yourself instinctively looking for 800 (or 500 when you are not vulnerable) to compensate. This means that you might overlook a defensive play needed simply to prevent the contract from making. Low-level contracts often prove the trickiest to defend accurately and not knowing what target to aim for only makes things worse.

At the table, the partner of one of the authors elected to leave in the double. East led a top club against Two Spades doubled. Then, placing West with four good spades and fearing club ruffs in dummy, he switched to a trump. Declarer could now have made the contract by finessing the queen of hearts, discarding a club on the heart ace and playing a diamond to the nine. In fact, reckoning that –200 would yield a good score anyway with 3NT cold for East-West, she decided to play safe for one down.

Leaving in Two Spades doubled constitutes a gross violation of the law of total tricks. If 2♡ promises six hearts, LHO may well hold seven spades to justify the rescue. Do you really want to defend at the two level when the opponents possess eight or nine trumps? If you cannot bring yourself to bid 3NT, you should cue-bid Three Spades, the suit in which your values lie. ***Not doubling them into game can spare you from straining for a big set at a low level.***

Love All   ♠ 10 4
Dealer East   ♡ 5 3
               ◇ J 9 7 6
               ♣ K 10 9 8 5

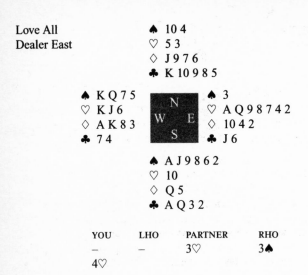

♠ K Q 7 5   ♠ 3
♡ K J 6   ♡ A Q 9 8 7 4 2
◇ A K 8 3   ◇ 10 4 2
♣ 7 4   ♣ J 6

               ♠ A J 9 8 6 2
               ♡ 10
               ◇ Q 5
               ♣ A Q 3 2

YOU	LHO	PARTNER	RHO
–	–	3♡	3♠
4♡			

Facing even a non-vulnerable pre-empt, this West hand looks rather good offensively. ♡K-J-x provides you with excellent support for a six- or, more likely, seven-card suit. The quick tricks in spades and diamonds are bound to come in handy, as might the doubleton club. If RHO passes over Three Hearts, you have an easy raise to game. Does his Three Spade overcall change anything?

RHO's action, whilst it marginally increases the danger of a bad trump break, significantly improves the chance that the ace of spades sits on your right or that partner turns up with a void spade. You would still count yourself unlucky if the heart game were to fail. How do you rate your defensive prospects?

You can reasonably expect to take four tricks, two in spades and two in diamonds. If partner produces the ace of hearts and nobody ruffs (or declarer loses control), Three Spades doubled will go down. Then again, if you find partner with the ace of hearts, Four Hearts will almost certainly be laydown. If you apply the law of total tricks, there may be ten hearts for your side and eight spades for theirs (partner figures to have a spade shortage, especially given your length and RHO's overcall). Therefore, with eighteen total tricks available, if Four Hearts fails, Three Spades makes. Whichever way you look at it, the decision is easy – doubling can hardly ever win. ***Not doubling them into game can enable you to go for your own best contract.***

East–West game
Dealer North

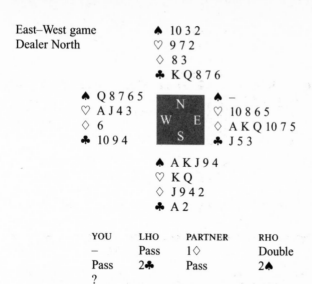

```
                         ♠ 10 3 2
                         ♡ 9 7 2
                         ◇ 8 3
                         ♣ K Q 8 7 6
        ♠ Q 8 7 6 5                      ♠ —
        ♡ A J 4 3          N             ♡ 10 8 6 5
        ◇ 6           W         E        ◇ A K Q 10 7 5
        ♣ 10 9 4           S             ♣ J 5 3
                         ♠ A K J 9 4
                         ♡ K Q
                         ◇ J 9 4 2
                         ♣ A 2
```

YOU	LHO	PARTNER	RHO
–	Pass	1◇	Double
Pass	2♣	Pass	2♠
?			

Okay, you might not open that East hand, but someone known as a normally cautious bidder did so at the table. Possibly, you would have acted on the previous round with your hand. Again, we can tell you that a famously aggressive player made the pass. However, he was unable to resist doubling when RHO pulled his Two Spade bid out of the bidding box. This would have made with an overtrick for 570 to North-South. Sensibly enough, knowing that West's inability to respond One Spade limited his spade holding, East removed the double to Three Diamonds. South had already shown a good hand by making a take-out double and then changing the suit, but he sensed his opponents were still in trouble and doubled 3◇. This resulted in a 200 point penalty – expensive on a part-score deal.

Think how differently events might turn out if West passes over Two Spades. North, who has promised nothing so far (the take-out double forced him to bid, remember), and who holds three trumps, a ruffing value and a source of tricks, would very probably raise the spades. If he jumps to game or if South goes on to Four Spades over a simple raise, then you could double. Trying for a penalty at the two level was ridiculous. *Not doubling them into game can allow your opponents to bid higher*.

On the last deal, we did not even bother to mention the danger of pushing the opponents into a better spot. If Two Spades actually was going down, they might well have retreated to Three Clubs. On our next offering, you do need to take account of such possibilities:

Game All
Dealer East

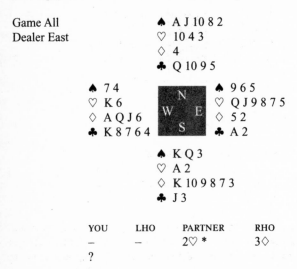

```
                    ♠ A J 10 8 2
                    ♡ 10 4 3
                    ◇ 4
                    ♣ Q 10 9 5
   ♠ 7 4                          ♠ 9 6 5
   ♡ K 6                          ♡ Q J 9 8 7 5
   ◇ A Q J 6                      ◇ 5 2
   ♣ K 8 7 6 4                    ♣ A 2
                    ♠ K Q 3
                    ♡ A 2
                    ◇ K 10 9 8 7 3
                    ♣ J 3
```

YOU	LHO	PARTNER	RHO
–	–	2♡ *	3◇
?			

Here partner's Weak Two has done its job: it forced the opponents to guess and they guessed wrong. Assuming that partner would avoid pre-empting in first or second seat with a four-card spade suit on the side, you can place the opponents with at least an eight-card spade fit. Even if he can open Two Hearts on an off-beat shape, it remains highly probable that the other side belongs in spades. By doubling Three Diamonds, you alert LHO to the fact that diamonds is not their best spot. Moreover you enable him to make a non-forcing Three Spade bid, an option he would very likely lack if you passed.

As the cards lie, you can easily defeat Three Diamonds by two tricks and collect 200. With either a diamond ruff or simple hold up beating the optimists in Four Hearts, this will give you a near top at pairs. If you greedily try for 500, LHO may run to the cold Three Spades. Worse still, putting you with more of an all-round defensive hand, partner may look at his three trumps and outside ace and double. Then you are well and truly up the creek. ***Not doubling them into game can prevent the enemy from running to a better spot.***

East–West game
Dealer North

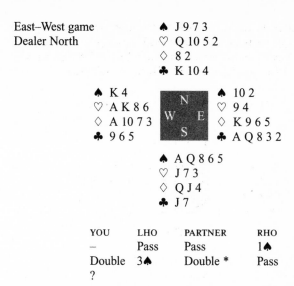

♠ J 9 7 3
♡ Q 10 5 2
◇ 8 2
♣ K 10 4

♠ K 4
♡ A K 8 6
◇ A 10 7 3
♣ 9 6 5

♠ 10 2
♡ 9 4
◇ K 9 6 5
♣ A Q 8 3 2

♠ A Q 8 6 5
♡ J 7 3
◇ Q J 4
♣ J 7

YOU	LHO	PARTNER	RHO
–	Pass	Pass	1♠
Double	3♠	Double *	Pass
?			

Opponents sometimes take liberties when you are vulnerable and they are not. This means you can find juicy pickings there for the taking. Here in fact they have hardly stretched; it just happens that both of them opted for the more aggressive of two possible actions on the same auction. First- or second-in-hand South would almost certainly refrain from opening; the two unsupported jacks are not pulling their full weight, the hand contains only about one and a half defensive tricks, and 5-3-3-2 is an uninspiring shape. However, many people play that you can open light in third seat. On the losing trick count, North's jump raise is marginal, but on the basis he would have raised to Two Spades without the double, it seems reasonable.

Partner's responsive double promises decent values since, if you take it out, you must either bid game (3NT) or at the four level. It also in principle denies four hearts – he would normally gamble on your holding support for the unbid major. Typically then, he will hold 9-11 points and 4-4 or 5-4 in the minors. Facing this you see little prospect of an eleven trick game, but your wealth of quick tricks suggests you can collect a worthwhile penalty. Indeed, assuming you give partner his heart ruff, you should score six top winners, the king of spades and a ruff for a whopping 800. ***Chance doubling them into game when a set seems sure but game for you appears unlikely.***

North–South game
Dealer East

♠ A K 7 5 4 3
♡ A 5
◇ K 9 4
♣ 10 2

♠ Q J 10 9 6
♡ 8
◇ A J 7 6
♣ A J 8

♠ 2
♡ K J 9 7 6 3 2
◇ 10 3
♣ Q 7 6

♠ 8
♡ Q 10 4
◇ Q 8 5 2
♣ K 9 5 4 3

YOU	LHO	PARTNER	RHO
–	–	3♡	Pass
Pass	3♠	Pass	Pass
?			

Here you have the wherewithal for a classic penalty double. Even
sitting under the bidder, a double can hardly ask for a take-out since
partner's pre-emptive opening has closely defined both the shape and
the strength of his hand. With your prospective defensive winners
consisting of aces and trump tricks, it would take an exceptionally freak
layout to allow declarer to scramble home in Three Spades doubled.
Even if one of the opponents unexpectedly turns up with a void in one
of the minors, partner could easily contribute a heart trick to
compensate. You also hold sufficiently good defensive values to deal
with an escape to 3NT or four of a minor. Indeed 3NT doubled can go
for 800, which is even better than the 500 you would collect defending
Three Spades Doubled.

Whilst we are not suggesting that your decision to double was
particularly close on this hand, we do wish to reiterate two important
points. Firstly, when partner makes a bid that indicates a strongly
offensive-orientated hand, assume he can contribute little against their
contract. Secondly, always take account of the possibility that an
opponent might turn up with a more distributional hand than he has
been able to get across. *Chance doubling them into game when your
trumps provide a safety margin.*

Game All
Dealer West

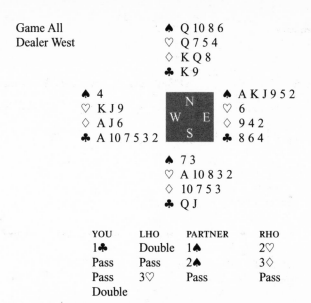

♠ Q 10 8 6
♡ Q 7 5 4
◇ K Q 8
♣ K 9

♠ 4
♡ K J 9
◇ A J 6
♣ A 10 7 5 3 2

♠ A K J 9 5 2
♡ 6
◇ 9 4 2
♣ 8 6 4

♠ 7 3
♡ A 10 8 3 2
◇ 10 7 5 3
♣ Q J

YOU	LHO	PARTNER	RHO
1♣	Double	1♠	2♡
Pass	Pass	2♠	3◇
Pass	3♡	Pass	Pass
Double			

For a vulnerable take-out double, the North hand seems definitely minimum. Still, as South could suggest any denomination and stay at the one-level, he scarcely expects to come to much harm. Partner's two spade bids and RHO's free bid of Two Hearts also look clear-cut. Arguably, you could have ventured Three Clubs over Two Hearts, but your singleton spade rightly induced you to prefer the more cautious pass. One can also offer considerable sympathy for South's Three Diamond rebid. He reckons on finding North with a fit in one if not both red suits. When, as here, he finds his partner with four-card heart support, he will rate the chance of getting doubled fairly low.

As it happens, you possess an extremely good hand defensively. As we said on the previous hand, aces always come in handy. In addition, your singleton spade looks good on several counts. For one thing, you might obtain a ruff or a trump promotion. For another, the fewer spades you hold, the greater the chance that partner's winners will stand up. Finally, it solves your opening lead problem. As the cards lie, you collect an easy 500 with neither opponent having done much wrong; just as on page 117 they have both taken marginally aggressive views on the same deal. ***Chance doubling them into game when having an attractive lead boosts your prospects.***

East–West game
Dealer East

```
                    ♠ K 7 4
                    ♡ 10 5
                    ♢ J 7 5 2
                    ♣ K 10 9 4
  ♠ Q 10 9 6                      ♠ –
  ♡ 6 2            N              ♡ A K J 7 4
  ♢ A K 8 4     W     E           ♢ 10 6 3
  ♣ 7 3 2          S              ♣ A Q 8 6 5
                    ♠ A J 8 5 3 2
                    ♡ Q 9 8 3
                    ♢ Q 9
                    ♣ J
```

YOU	LHO	PARTNER	RHO
–	–	1♡	1♠
1NT	2♠	3♣	3♠
?			

Maybe your opponents are not playing weak jump overcalls, or perhaps South judged the hand too good. Be that as it may, RHO's actions look fairly reasonable given the vulnerability. He knows that his side can lay claim up to at least a nine-card spade fit. So, following general total tricks principles, he competes to the three level. Indeed, his 6-4-2-1 shape appears to give him a margin for error. Unluckily for him, the North-South hands happen to fit poorly, with almost all their high cards wasted. Can you tell this from the West seat?

Since you might pass first time expecting partner to reopen on many hands, your 1NT response promised 7-9 points and a stopper in spades. If anything, the later bidding has improved your hand – if you can avoid becoming dummy. South, who bid spades twice, is likely to hold the jack, giving you two spade tricks. In addition, with hearts and clubs bid by East, your two top diamonds rate to score. With maybe four tricks in your hand and partner promising a better than minimum opening, punting 3NT remains a possibility. However, even allowing for the vulnerability, it seems better to double. With the misfit, you cannot guarantee nine tricks in 3NT despite having the balance of power, but you are very hopeful of five defending. Three Spades doubled nets 500 whilst 3NT would fail. *Chance doubling them into game when you have power on a misfit hand*.

East–West game

Dealer North

♠ K Q 7 6 5 4
♡ K 7
◇ K 4
♣ K 8 4

♠ J 10 8 3 2
♡ 6 5
◇ A 9 6 5
♣ 10 3

♠ A 9
♡ A Q 10 3
◇ J 7 3
♣ A Q 9 2

♠ —
♡ J 9 8 4 2
◇ Q 10 8 2
♣ J 7 6 5

YOU	LHO	PARTNER	RHO
–	1♠	Double	Pass
2◇	2♠	Pass	Pass
?			

We mentioned on the first page of the chapter that spurning the chance of a penalty double (or penalty pass) on one round still allows you to go for the jugular on the next. Here we see a case in point. To leave the double of One Spade in, you would require faster spade tricks. If North turns up with A-K-Q-x-x, it might prove very difficult to keep him from scoring all five of them. Now that the bidding has come back and again the opportunity presents itself to express an opinion about the likelihood of his success in a spade contract, you can safely double. The fact that you took out One Spade doubled warns partner against placing you with a spade stack. Furthermore, the knowledge that you hold a diamond suit of sorts gives him an easy escape route if he does not fancy his chances defending. When in practice he passes, it saves him a headache about what to lead.

Here you struck lucky, catching partner with a hand that almost justified action by him over 2♠ (indeed his correct call if he were not passing was double – this is the wrong type of spade holding for a 2NT bid). Nonetheless, even if you give him a weaker hand, maybe swapping his ace of spades with North's four, you could get it two off. *Chance doubling them into game when partner should know if it needs taking out.*

Lest you get carried away with your success on the last few examples, we had better finish by reminding you of an additional reason to exercise caution in making low-level doubles. Whereas a double at high level can put declarer under added pressure, a 'double into game' invariably increases the strain on the defenders. How often have you seen a defending side fail to collect one of the five or six tricks rightfully theirs? In our experience, this happens quite often, even at the top level of the game. If declarer has been given a free shot at game, and can see himself going no more than one down, he can play the hand with his normal relaxed attitude. When, however, the defending side knows that the slightest slip can result in a bottom at pairs or an even greater disaster at other forms of scoring, the high stakes can distract them from their task.

Golden Rule Eleven:

Not Doubling Them into Game can

. . . Save you from needlessly conceding a game;
. . . Spare you from straining for a big set at a low level;
. . . Enable you to go for your own best contract;
. . . Allow your opponents to bid higher;
. . . Prevent the enemy from running to a better spot.

Chance Doubling Them into Game when

. . . A set seems sure but game for you appears unlikely;
. . . Your trumps provide a safety margin;
. . . Having an attractive lead boosts your prospects;
. . . You have power on a misfit hand;
. . . Partner should know if it needs taking out.

Rule Twelve: Beware of Free Doubles

Since turning a part-score into game with a double has such a taboo associated with it, other doubles have gained the term 'free doubles'. In practice, doubles of contracts below two of a major or of those at game and slam level are anything but free. Whilst the double does not affect the award of a game bonus, it still doubles the trick score and the 50 for insult applies just the same. Again, the odds work against close doubles. The worst sort are those that enable declarer to place the cards and make a contract that would ordinarily fail.

Game All
Dealer South

	♠ J 10 3	
	♡ A K Q 5	
	◇ A K 8	
	♣ K 7 4	

♠ K Q 4		♠ 5
♡ J 10 8 6		♡ 9 4 3
◇ 9 7 3		◇ 6 5 4 2
♣ J 9 6		♣ Q 10 8 5 2

	♠ A 9 8 7 6 2	
	♡ 7 2	
	◇ Q J 10	
	♣ A 3	

YOU	LHO	PARTNER	RHO
–	–	–	1♠
Pass	2♡	Pass	2♠
Pass	4NT *	Pass	5♡ *
Pass	6♠	Pass	Pass
?			

Here it is vital to know what to do since a slow pass may prove just as costly as a double. Indeed, Rixi Markus once made a similar slam on a trump endplay because West was looking rather happier than one might expect (ruff a heart and a club in hand, cash all other side-suit winners and exit with a spade at trick eleven). ***Bewaring of free doubles can avoid warning declarer of a bad break***.

Love All
Dealer South

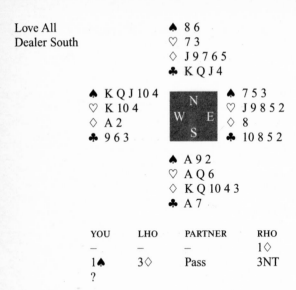

```
                    ♠ 8 6
                    ♡ 7 3
                    ◇ J 9 7 6 5
                    ♣ K Q J 4
   ♠ K Q J 10 4                      ♠ 7 5 3
   ♡ K 10 4            N             ♡ J 9 8 5 2
   ◇ A 2          W         E        ◇ 8
   ♣ 9 6 3            S             ♣ 10 8 5 2
                    ♠ A 9 2
                    ♡ A Q 6
                    ◇ K Q 10 4 3
                    ♣ A 7
```

YOU	LHO	PARTNER	RHO
–	–	–	1◇
1♠	3◇	Pass	3NT
?			

Your opponents brush aside your One Spade overcall and steam into the no-trump game, North's jump raise to Three Diamonds being largely pre-emptive in nature. Can you resist doubling?

For sure, you fancy your chances here. It appears unlikely that North possesses five spades and even more improbable that South does. Adding this to the fact that you have the ace of diamonds, a suit declarer seems set to play on, you can feel confident of beating the contract. Moreover, your king of hearts sitting over the strong hand may yield a sixth defensive trick. Looking at a sure one-trick set and a shot at a 300 penalty, can you believe we want you to pass?

If you double, both opponents get the opportunity to reconsider the wisdom of playing in no-trumps. If North retreats to 4◇, South will raise to the diamond game, which is stone cold. In an attempt to increase the penalty from 50 to 100 in 3NT, you risk the loss of 450 points (the 50 you would collect from 3NT undoubled down one and the 400 you lose from Five Diamonds making). Except at match-point pairs or similar forms of scoring, the odds thus come out at 9:1 against you. To justify the double you would either need an auction that made it less possible the opponents would run – or else better defensive prospects against their alternative game. ***Bewaring of free doubles can stop your opponents from finding a better spot.***

Game All
Dealer East

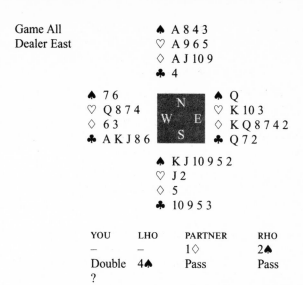

```
                    ♠ A 8 4 3
                    ♡ A 9 6 5
                    ◇ A J 10 9
                    ♣ 4
    ♠ 7 6                          ♠ Q
    ♡ Q 8 7 4          N           ♡ K 10 3
    ◇ 6 3          W       E       ◇ K Q 8 7 4 2
    ♣ A K J 8 6        S           ♣ Q 7 2
                    ♠ K J 10 9 5 2
                    ♡ J 2
                    ◇ 5
                    ♣ 10 9 5 3
```

YOU	LHO	PARTNER	RHO
–	–	1◇	2♠
Double	4♠	Pass	Pass
?			

When you hold around 10 points and partner opens the bidding, you expect your side to buy the contract. When the opponents outbid you, your thoughts naturally turn to thinking of what penalty may be on offer. On this hand, you have two possible club winners. If you count these as well as the normal expectation of defensive winners for a minimum opening bid, two tricks, you would hope to defeat the contract more often than not. Still, you gave partner a fair picture of your values by making a negative double that invited him to rebid at the 3-level. You can hardly claim to offer a lot extra. In addition, your opponents can see the vulnerability and will not hold tram tickets. Again, examination of the mathematics proves conclusive . . .

If you double and beat Four Spades by a trick, you increase the penalty from 100 to 200, a gain of 100. If, however, Four Spades doubled makes, the opponents score 790 instead of 620, a loss of 170. To break even you would need to expect to defeat the contract at least 63% of the time. In practice, the danger of an overtrick or a redouble makes the odds worse. Bearing in mind that your hand may contribute zero tricks if an opponent turns up with a void club, this would constitute a rash double even at pairs. Partner has already turned down the chance to double and you should not override him. ***Bewaring of free doubles can keep your minus to a minimum***.

Game All
Dealer North

Using an old-fashioned Baron sequence, your opponents launch themselves into the no-trump slam. You have two certain winners, but unfortunately not the opening lead. Do you double?

Generally speaking, doubles of slams involve more risk than usual. For one thing, the opponents tend to have a good idea of their combined assets when they get up to the six- or seven-level. For another, if a double jostles them out of a failing contract into a making one or enables them to find a winning line they would normally miss, the loss becomes huge. Furthermore, since the trick score itself is higher than at lower levels, the numbers come out more strongly against the doubler. If you convert 100 into 200, you gain 100 points. By contrast, if they make 6NT, you convert their 1440 into 1680, a loss of 240 points. Since the odds are stacked against slam doubles, they often assume lead-directing connotations. Here a double would ask for a spade lead, dummy's suit. In the absence of double, partner will tend to lead a diamond more often than anything else (remember you failed to double 3♣). Without a diamond lead, a danger exists that declarer can run four tricks in every other suit and scrape home. With this hand, you would need to be on lead to double. ***Bewaring of free doubles can encourage partner to lead an unbid suit***.

East–West game
Dealer West

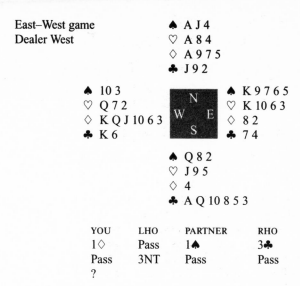

		♠ A J 4	
		♡ A 8 4	
		◇ A 9 7 5	
		♣ J 9 2	

♠ 10 3
♡ Q 7 2
◇ K Q J 10 6 3
♣ K 6

♠ K 9 7 6 5
♡ K 10 6 3
◇ 8 2
♣ 7 4

♠ Q 8 2
♡ J 9 5
◇ 4
♣ A Q 10 8 5 3

YOU	LHO	PARTNER	RHO
1◇	Pass	1♠	3♣
Pass	3NT	Pass	Pass
?			

Although you hold a minimum for your opening bid, you rate your chance of beating 3NT as high. You know declarer will need to develop the clubs, and your king of clubs will provide an entry if, as expected, the ace lies with the long suit on your right. Moreover, as you have not raised spades (or suggested a partial fit with a support double), you should feel confident that partner will lead your suit. Another positive factor for raising the stakes is that if 3NT goes down, it will probably go two down, giving you 300.

Now we need to consider the risks accompanying a double. Firstly, declarer may turn up with a 5-card diamond suit, which could give him a double stopper. Secondly, the ace of clubs may sit over your king, which would snuff out both your entry to your diamonds and your club stopper. Thirdly, if the opponents have misjudged and 3NT is doomed to failure, someone may run to Four Clubs, which you are unlikely to beat. However, a more compelling reason exists than any of these to refrain from doubling: in the absence of a contrary agreement, a double carries a lead-directing message – lead your suit partner, not mine. The logic stands out: without a double partner would normally lead your suit. This makes his suit the unusual lead, something you must avoid asking for on this hand. ***Bewaring of free doubles can ensure partner leads your suit***.

Up until now we have kept finding reasons why you should resist the temptation to double your opponents. As you would expect, times must come when you should pull out a red card. You need to deter injudicious adverse bidding and collect gifts when they are on offer. Let us consider our first 'rule breaking' example:

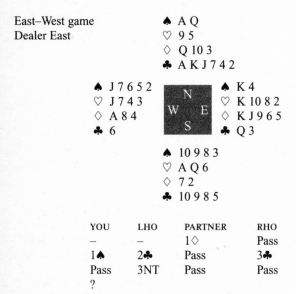

East–West game
Dealer East

<table>
<tr><td>YOU</td><td>LHO</td><td>PARTNER</td><td>RHO</td></tr>
<tr><td>–</td><td>–</td><td>1♦</td><td>Pass</td></tr>
<tr><td>1♠</td><td>2♣</td><td>Pass</td><td>3♣</td></tr>
<tr><td>Pass</td><td>3NT</td><td>Pass</td><td>Pass</td></tr>
<tr><td>?</td><td></td><td></td><td></td></tr>
</table>

We have given you a couple of deals on which we warned against doubling if you wanted partner to make his normal lead and a double would deflect him from it. Here the converse applies.

You lack a club stopper, but this is hardly a big issue. Indeed your singleton may herald a bad break and, since declarer holds both more strength and more clubs than dummy, any club finesse for him figures to lose. The key point on this hand is the disparity in strength between your spades and diamonds. Your ace of diamonds could come as a very pleasant surprise to partner if he attacks the suit, whilst your spade holding means that a spade lead may well blow a trick. To tell partner that you prefer a diamond, his suit, you double. This enables you to defeat a contract that might otherwise make and therefore gains not just 50 points (100–50), but 500 (100+400). ***Make a free double when you want partner's suit to be led***.

East–West game
Dealer North

	♠ A J 9 6 5
	♡ A Q 8
	◇ 9 4 3
	♣ Q 2

West:
♠ 10 7 4
♡ 10 9 6 4 3
◇ —
♣ A 8 7 6 5

East:
♠ 3
♡ J 7 5
◇ J 7 5 2
♣ K J 10 9 4

South:
♠ K Q 8 2
♡ K 2
◇ A K Q 10 8 6
♣ 3

YOU	LHO	PARTNER	RHO
–	1♠	Pass	3◇
Pass	3♠	Pass	4NT *
Pass	5♡ *	Pass	6♠
?			

We offer our apologies if you think we ought now to conclude our coverage of lead-directing doubles. It really is such an important weapon to have that we almost cannot include too many.

Looking at this West hand, you can see a virtually sure-fire way to defeat Six Spades. Given that RHO would not use an ace enquiry with a void, there is every chance that you can ruff a diamond at trick one and cash a club at trick two. Indeed, if partner leads a very low diamond and you can interpret it as a suit-preference signal, you can underlead the club ace at trick two and obtain a second ruff. Luckily, you have a way to persuade partner to lead a diamond: double. This is a Lightner double and asks for an unusual lead, normally the first suit bid by dummy. Okay, a slight risk exists that the opponents can safely retreat to 6NT (not that they can on this deal). In this event, assuming partner would not have found the diamond lead, you have lost almost nothing. In the actual scenario you turn –980 into +300.

Next time he holds a hand like this South will bid 4NT directly over his partner's opening bid. Of course, if you had the same hand, you would still double the final contract, suggesting a void somewhere, but partner would then have to figure out where it is. ***Make a free double when you desire a lead of one of their suits***.

♠ 6 4	YOU	LHO	PARTNER	RHO
♡ A 9 6 4	Pass	1NT	Pass	2◇ *
◇ K Q 10 7 3	?			
♣ 8 2				

In this situation, it makes no difference what strength no-trump the opponents play. Having passed as dealer, a double of RHO's transfer into hearts can only mean one thing, diamonds. At this stage in the auction, you cannot tell if they will end up in a suit or a no-trump contract. Therefore, you need both length and strength in diamonds – otherwise you cannot know whether you want the suit led. We certainly advise you to have a five-card suit; with anything less, you could wind up defending Two Diamonds Redoubled with alarming regularity. Of course, you hardly need restrict this type of double to the specific case of a transfer. Provided RHO's 2◇ call is artificial, forcing Stayman perhaps, your double shows diamonds. *Make a free double when you want to double a conventional call for the lead*.

Next we consider what a double of a suit you have already bid should mean. After all, you would generally expect partner to lead it. Sadly, it is difficult to supply a hard and fast rule. Take this auction:

YOU	LHO	PARTNER	RHO
1♣	1NT	Pass	2♣ *
Double			

If RHO's 2♣ is simple Stayman, he may have a bust and you could have a good hand, in which case double might show extra values. If instead 2♣ is a game-forcing cue bid, this would be an inefficient use of the call. In this case, double should probably retain its usual meaning of asking for a club lead. After all, in many systems a One Club opening may be only a 3- or 4-card suit, and partner will often look elsewhere when LHO has announced strength in the suit.

However, life may not be quite so simple. If your bid promised length in the suit whilst implying that you could not have the values to compete at the level the auction is now at, you may want a double to say 'please do not lead my suit.' For example, the bidding could go 3♣ from you, 3♡ from LHO, pass by partner, 4♣ by RHO.

We advise that in these types of auction you should only double if you feel confident that partner will correctly read your intentions.

You may be pleased to hear that we now proceed to take a break from doubles of the lead-directing variety and return to those of the good old-fashioned 'they've made a mistake' type.

Game All
Dealer South

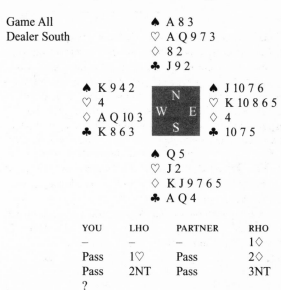

```
                    ♠ A 8 3
                    ♡ A Q 9 7 3
                    ◇ 8 2
                    ♣ J 9 2
    ♠ K 9 4 2                      ♠ J 10 7 6
    ♡ 4                            ♡ K 10 8 6 5
    ◇ A Q 10 3                     ◇ 4
    ♣ K 8 6 3                      ♣ 10 7 5
                    ♠ Q 5
                    ♡ J 2
                    ◇ K J 9 7 6 5
                    ♣ A Q 4
```

YOU	LHO	PARTNER	RHO
–	–	–	1◇
Pass	1♡	Pass	2◇
Pass	2NT	Pass	3NT
?			

What clues does this auction give you? RHO's simple repeat of his suit suggests a minimum opening and his raise of 2NT to 3NT indicates only a fraction extra. The premium attached to a vulnerable game at teams and rubber means that players require little excuse to accept an invitation. Whilst LHO's One Heart response could have concealed a monster, his 2NT rebid limits his hand to around 10-12 points. Therefore, neither opponent can hold reserves of values. From your hand, you can tell that both red suits are lying badly for declarer, with the suits splitting unevenly and finesses surely failing. Moreover, you can tolerate any of partner's likely opening leads. This all makes the conditions ideal for a speculative penalty double.

With RHO having bid diamonds twice, your double does not request a diamond lead, although you could stand one. Indeed, you can get 800 on a diamond lead. Better still, if partner leads a normal spade, you should collect 1100. *Make a free double when their values sound limited and the breaks are bad.*

Our next example contains a number of similar features, and some new factors enter into the equation:

North–South game
Dealer South

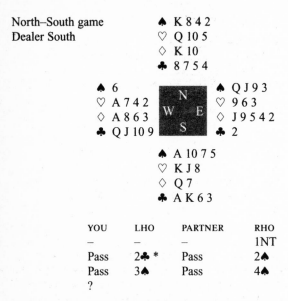

```
                      ♠ K 8 4 2
                      ♡ Q 10 5
                      ♦ K 10
                      ♣ 8 7 5 4
        ♠ 6                          ♠ Q J 9 3
        ♡ A 7 4 2          N         ♡ 9 6 3
        ♦ A 8 6 3     W         E    ♦ J 9 5 4 2
        ♣ Q J 10 9         S         ♣ 2
                      ♠ A 10 7 5
                      ♡ K J 8
                      ♦ Q 7
                      ♣ A K 6 3
```

YOU	LHO	PARTNER	RHO
–	–	–	1NT
Pass	2♣ *	Pass	2♠
Pass	3♠	Pass	4♠
?			

Beginning with a strong no-trump opening and a simple Stayman response, your opponents arrive in the spade game. Hearing this sequence, how do you feel about the defensive prospects?

RHO's opening limits his hand to 15-17 and LHO's invitational 3♠ limits his. Once more, you can tell that they lack any values to spare. In addition, they have only shown one suit and you can judge from your singleton that this is breaking badly. The fact that they use ordinary Stayman rather than 5-card suggests they seldom open 1NT with a 5-card major, and North might have preferred a transfer if he held five. This makes it likely partner will produce four trumps.

Other positive features defensively include your pair of aces and an attractive opening lead. A bonus comes if declarer misreads the lie of the cards because of your double. With no double, he will surely attack trumps by leading the king first and escape for one down: 100. After the double, he may well start with the ace and generate an extra trump loser; then you rake in 500. *Make a free double when doing so may induce declarer to misplace the cards*.

Game All
Dealer East

	♠ Q 5
	♡ J 5
	◇ K Q 9 7 6 5
	♣ Q 10 4

♠ 10 8 6 4   ♠ A K 9 7 3 2
♡ 10 7 3   ♡ A 9 4
◇ A J 8 4   ◇ 10 2
♣ K 6   ♣ 8 2

♠ J
♡ K Q 8 6 2
◇ 3
♣ A J 9 7 5 3

YOU	LHO	PARTNER	RHO
–	–	1♠	2♠ *
3♠	5◇	Pass	Pass
?			

LHO alerted Two Spades and the opponents' convention card says this should show a two-suited hand with the reds. It is of course possible that nothing untoward has happened, partner holding a void diamond and LHO taking a flyer with no spades and 4-card diamond support. However, you can sense RHO feeling a little uneasy.

As a first move, you should ask about the 2♠ bid. If you misread their system card, this may protect you from doing anything foolish. Moreover, if RHO forgot the system, he cannot ethically 'remember' it on the basis of any explanation. With four decent trumps, an outside king and an opening bid from your partner, you would probably be prepared to gamble a double at the five level anyway. In practice, it yields a bonanza, Five Diamonds doubled going for 1100. If it was North who had the system wrong (evidently having brought the wrong convention card), he would be entitled to remove the double if he recollects the true agreement. In this case, you would still collect 500 from Five Hearts Doubled or 800 from Six Clubs Doubled. Four Spades would make your way if RHO leads the ♡K (or ♣A), but his singleton diamond or, less likely, a low heart would beat it. A deal just like this occurred in the 1983 Varsity match. Having lost 1100 on the previous board as well, Oxford never recovered their morale. *Make a free double when you suspect a wheel has come off*.

♠ 10 6 4	YOU	LHO	PARTNER	RHO
♡ 9 7 3	–	–	2♣ *	Pass
◇ 9 8 6 2	2◇ *	4♠	Pass	Pass
♣ 10 7 4	?			

With hands like this, bidding problems rarely surface: you pass throughout and hope partner stays out of trouble. Well, this time, you cannot bury your head in the sand. Partner's nominally game-forcing Two Club opening makes his pass over LHO's 4♠ forcing. No matter how much you hate it, you must do something. By inference partner must have a distributional hand and visions of making a high-level contract – with a balanced hand he would double Four Spades to keep you quiet. Armed with this information, what do you do?

Assuming you will not take a trick in any event, you need to judge if partner will have a greater chance of making ten or eleven tricks with his choice of trumps or four with theirs. This is easy. You double. He can always take it out if he has enormous playing strength.

♠ 4 2	YOU	LHO	PARTNER	RHO
♡ K 10 6	–	–	1♡	1♠
◇ A Q 9 4	2♠ *	3♠	4♡	4♠
♣ Q 10 7 2	?			

For the sake of argument, we will say that your side alone is vulnerable on this deal. From your hand and the auction to date you can guess that partner's One Heart opening promised five: otherwise you would prefer a negative double to the cue bid or, if that were not available, a change-of-suit response in one of your minors. Where does this leave you over Four Spades?

Partner has made an opening bid and gone on to game, whilst you have promised high-card values as well as at least three-card heart support. Putting all these factors together and, if you think it makes a difference on your methods, the adverse vulnerability, it sounds like the opponents are sacrificing. Therefore, if you pass, partner will construe it as forcing, an invitation to bid on. With only three trumps, no extra values and the worst possible spade length, this is the last thing you want to do. To warn him that your hand appears unsuitable for a foray to the 5-level you should double. *Make a free double when the auction has made a pass forcing*.

♠ Q 8 7 6	YOU	LHO	PARTNER	RHO
♡ –	–	–	3♡	3NT
◊ K Q J 10 8	?			
♣ A J 7 6				

On occasion you can tell that a possibly normal action by an opponent figures to work badly. In this situation, you need to extract the maximum. Many will be the time when, in accordance with rule 5, RHO will venture an overcall hoping that this partner turns up with about 8 points. Since he will score well through adopting this policy most of the time, you need to make the most of it when his luck is out. You expect to take five tricks in your own hand: four diamonds and the club ace. Partner may well have a heart trick, and if he has bits and pieces such as the spade jack or the club ten, these would bolster your holdings. Finally, with your three-suited hand, you hardly need fear that your quarry will find safety in a 4-level suit contract. *Make a free double when you are very confident of a set.*

♠ 9 7 6 4	YOU	LHO	PARTNER	RHO
♡ J 8 6 3	–	–	3♡	4♠
◊ 8 2	?			
♣ J 7 2				

Unless you play an exceptionally strong style of pre-emptive openings, you expect the opponents to have a slam, maybe a grand slam. We see this as more of a tactical decision than a technical one, and various strategies may work. You could bid Five Hearts, killing all of LHO's slam-try options at the 5-level. Alternatively, you might try a psychic 4NT. Sadly, you hold too little to believe the other side will take this seriously. On occasion, a pre-emptive raise to 6♡ or 7♡ could also win the day, forcing opponents to guess at a high level. A double also sounds an interesting possibility. Four Spades Doubled with two overtricks scores 790 or 1190, rather less than Six Spades bid and made (980 or 1430). Of course, if somebody redoubles, you will turn tail and retreat to Five Hearts. The pre-planned escape has given this double a name: a striped-tailed ape, after the stripe-tailed lemur of Madagascar, which, while strictly speaking not an ape, is a nervous creature. *Make a free double when you want to keep the enemy out of a slam and you have an escape.*

North–South game
Dealer West

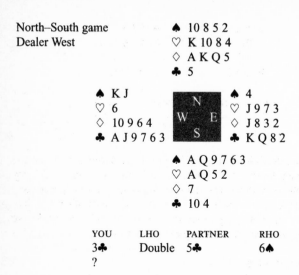

```
                        ♠ 10 8 5 2
                        ♡ K 10 8 4
                        ◇ A K Q 5
                        ♣ 5
        ♠ K J                             ♠ 4
        ♡ 6                               ♡ J 9 7 3
        ◇ 10 9 6 4       N                ◇ J 8 3 2
        ♣ A J 9 7 6 3   W   E             ♣ K Q 8 2
                          S
                        ♠ A Q 9 7 6 3
                        ♡ A Q 5 2
                        ◇ 7
                        ♣ 10 4
```

YOU	LHO	PARTNER	RHO
3♣	Double	5♣	6♠
?			

For a non-vulnerable pre-empt, your hand offers great defensive prospects. You hold the ace of your suit, clubs, and the fact that you have only a six-card suit means there is a realistic chance it will stand up. Moreover, your spade holding looks like a more or less certain trick. Surely South will have the ace or queen of spades to jump to a slam in the suit at least nine times out of ten. As we discussed earlier, you would not double an opposing slam just because you saw a reasonable expectation of defeating the contract and sought to change 100 into 200: if the opponents go down, you are on to a good thing anyway. Here a new factor comes into the reckoning.

With the other side alone vulnerable, partner may well hold a hand on which he believes a sacrifice will cost rather less than their slam. If so, and you pass at this juncture, he will bid Seven Clubs (unless he worries that the opponents might bid and make Seven Spades). To prevent this from happening you need to double.

Note that some expert pairs use a device known as an 'unpenalty' double. This applies when it sounds as if a save will be cheap and helps you to assess whether the enemy slam will make. Playing this, double says, 'I have no defensive trick' whilst pass means you think you do. Partner then judges whether to save. This works well when you each have a trick, but would not help here. *Make a free double when you cannot take the risk that partner might sacrifice.*

	♠ A K Q 9 8 6	♠ J 2	
	♡ 10 5	♡ J 7 6 2	
	◇ J 3	◇ 9 5 2	
	♣ 5 4 3	♣ Q 8 7 2	

YOU	LHO	PARTNER	RHO
–	1NT	Pass	3NT
Double			

Ordinarily a lead-directing double asks for a particular suit and, if you agree what the suit is, typically one of the majors, you could play that in this situation. If not, your double simply says 'I have a very good suit over here, partner – please try to find it.' He does this by leading his shortest suit, preferring a major if he is in doubt. *Make a free double when you need partner to guess your suit.*

Golden Rule Twelve:

Bewaring of Free Doubles can

. . . Avoid warning declarer of a bad break;
. . . Stop your opponents from finding a better spot;
. . . Keep your minus to a minimum;
. . . Encourage partner to lead an unbid suit;
. . . Ensure partner leads your suit.

Make a Free Double when

. . . You want partner's suit to be led;
. . . You desire a lead of one of their suits;
. . . You want to double a conventional call for the lead;
. . . Their values sound limited and the breaks are bad;
. . . Doing so might induce declarer to misplace the cards;
. . . You suspect a wheel has come off;
. . . The auction has made a pass forcing;
. . . You are very confident of a set;
. . . You want to keep them out of slam and have an escape;
. . . You cannot take the risk that partner might sacrifice;
. . . You need partner to guess your suit.

Rule Thirteen: Pass Partner's Penalty Doubles

If partner adheres to the two previous rules and allows a margin of safety with his penalty doubles, you will rarely need to take them out. Only when your hand differs markedly from what your previous bidding suggested should you elect to run. Even then, you need to have a positive idea of where you want to go. You may expect little sympathy if a juicy penalty goes begging or your side gets doubled.

North–South game
Dealer West

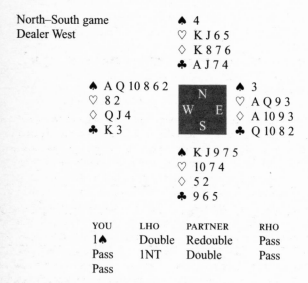

	♠ 4
	♡ K J 6 5
	◇ K 8 7 6
	♣ A J 7 4

♠ A Q 10 8 6 2   ♠ 3
♡ 8 2   ♡ A Q 9 3
◇ Q J 4   ◇ A 10 9 3
♣ K 3   ♣ Q 10 8 2

♠ K J 9 7 5
♡ 10 7 4
◇ 5 2
♣ 9 6 5

YOU	LHO	PARTNER	RHO
1♠	Double	Redouble	Pass
Pass	1NT	Double	Pass
Pass			

Partner's redouble suggests a desire to punish the opponents and his double of LHO's retreat to 1NT reinforces the message. With a sound opening bid, and being very happy to see your suit led, you should pass in your sleep. Indeed, you can collect a whopping 1100 on a spade lead. You do just as well if LHO tries an SOS redouble. Two Clubs Doubled and Two Hearts Doubled go four down as well. If you pull the double to Two Spades, partner may think you opened light and pass. Then you do not even get game! *Passing partner's penalty doubles can allow you to collect a useful penalty*.

North–South game
Dealer West

```
                        ♠ 4
                        ♡ K Q 9 7 6 4
                        ◇ A K 8 6
                        ♣ Q 6
        ♠ K J 10 9 6 5 3          ♠ 7
        ♡ 8              N        ♡ A J 10 2
        ◇ Q 7 2       W   E      ◇ 10 4 3
        ♣ 10 3          S        ♣ A K 8 4 2
                        ♠ A Q 8 2
                        ♡ 5 3
                        ◇ J 9 5
                        ♣ J 9 7 5
```

YOU	LHO	PARTNER	RHO
3♠	4♡	Double	Pass
Pass			

This time your hand lacks any defensive values but again you should pass contentedly. You announced that your hand would play much better in spades than in anything else when you made your pre-emptive opening. Partner, having heard this, has expressed a definite opinion that LHO has chosen the wrong moment to enter the auction. Because your opening bid defined your hand so well, there is no need to doubt partner's intentions. You have told your story. Just thank your fairy godmother that partner holds such a good hand and that you can contribute both a trump and the queen of diamonds. Remember, you never promised either of these cards.

As the cards lie, both major-suit games go two down. In Four Hearts Doubled, declarer has to lose three trumps and two clubs. Indeed, he requires an endplay to avoid a diamond loser and restrict the penalty to 500. If you mistakenly bid Four Spades, a clear case of bidding your hand twice, South might well double. Unless perhaps you manage to fool North into playing a second round of diamonds through dropping the seven on the first round, you will lose three diamonds and two trumps to concede 300. To say that partner and, if you have them, team-mates will be displeased sounds something of an understatement. *Passing partner's penalty doubles can avoid turning a plus into a minus*.

East–West game
Dealer North

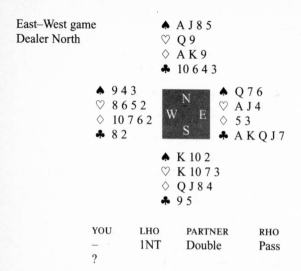

```
                ♠ A J 8 5
                ♡ Q 9
                ◇ A K 9
                ♣ 10 6 4 3

♠ 9 4 3                         ♠ Q 7 6
♡ 8 6 5 2          N            ♡ A J 4
◇ 10 7 6 2     W       E        ◇ 5 3
♣ 8 2              S            ♣ A K Q J 7

                ♠ K 10 2
                ♡ K 10 7 3
                ◇ Q J 8 4
                ♣ 9 5
```

YOU	LHO	PARTNER	RHO
–	1NT	Double	Pass
?			

Here you have a lousy hand, but on this occasion partner may not know it. Assuming that LHO's 1NT opening shows 12-14, the double indicates anything from 15 points upwards. If partner lies at the lower end of the range, he will most probably be hoping that you turn up with a fair share of the missing values. If this is the case, he will be sorely disappointed. Looking on the bright side, however, it seems perfectly possible that he can beat the contract in his own hand. He might have a rock crusher or a good suit to attack coupled with a few entries. Most experts recommend that you should pass a penalty double of 1NT on any balanced hand. Do you see why?

If partner holds a minimum for his double, your side is in trouble whatever you do. RHO will know his side owns the balance of power and will double your escape. Furthermore, holding only four card suits, you have absolutely no guarantee of finding a decent fit. If you guess to play the hand in Two Diamonds Doubled, you may go five off and have to write down 1400 in the minus column. Two Hearts Doubled fares little better. The penalty there is 'only' 1100. Partner would do best to take you out to Three Clubs, but how can he guess that you are playing Russian roulette by introducing four card suits? 1NT doubled does not score game – cut your losses and pass. The resulting –180 is scarcely a disaster. ***Passing partner's penalty doubles can save you from conceding a large number***.

East–West game
Dealer East

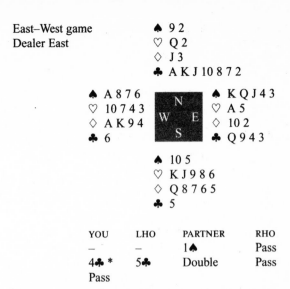

♠ 9 2
♡ Q 2
◇ J 3
♣ A K J 10 8 7 2

♠ A 8 7 6
♡ 10 7 4 3
◇ A K 9 4
♣ 6

♠ K Q J 4 3
♡ A 5
◇ 10 2
♣ Q 9 4 3

♠ 10 5
♡ K J 9 8 6
◇ Q 8 7 6 5
♣ 5

YOU	LHO	PARTNER	RHO
–	–	1♠	Pass
4♣ *	5♣	Double	Pass
Pass			

Sometimes you feel like wringing an opponent's neck when he sacrifices against your side's game contract. You own the hand; why should you have to defend? You really want to play the hand or, if you are dummy, go out for a quick smoke or chat up the barmaid or whatever. Nonetheless, if you want to win at bridge, you will need to control these emotional reactions. At the end of the day, going home having won the match or with money in your wallet will surely bring more satisfaction.

Okay, you hold a singleton club but you made that crystal clear with your Splinter bid of Four Clubs. Partner's double means one of two things: either an express desire to defend or merely a wish not to have to look for eleven tricks. Holding three defensive tricks and no extra shape or slam interest it would be barmy to overrule his decision. As the cards lie, partner can make Five Spades even on a trump lead if he plays it carefully. However, you would far rather collect a four-figure penalty. Against Five Clubs doubled, you can cash your top winners and then play a third round of diamonds to promote the nine of clubs. 1100 would surely yield a top at pairs and would produce an 11-IMP swing at teams. At rubber or Chicago for big bucks, it would be sweeter still! *Passing partner's penalty doubles can give you the chance of a bonanza.*

East–West game
Dealer North

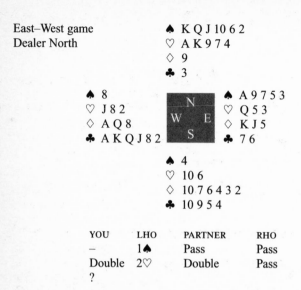

```
                        ♠ K Q J 10 6 2
                        ♡ A K 9 7 4
                        ◇ 9
                        ♣ 3
        ♠ 8                          ♠ A 9 7 5 3
        ♡ J 8 2              N        ♡ Q 5 3
        ◇ A Q 8         W        E    ◇ K J 5
        ♣ A K Q J 8 2        S        ♣ 7 6
                        ♠ 4
                        ♡ 10 6
                        ◇ 10 7 6 4 3 2
                        ♣ 10 9 5 4
```

YOU	LHO	PARTNER	RHO
–	1♠	Pass	Pass
Double	2♡	Double	Pass
?			

In the direct position, you would have chosen to make a simple Two Club overcall (unless you play strong jump overcalls, which hardly anybody does these days). In the balancing seat, where you mentally add a king to your values, you were absolutely right to start with a double.

With one opponent bidding by himself, partner's double is not responsive (and the same would apply if North were repeating his suit). It means business. Still, it seems unlikely partner has a heart stack. He would expect you to hold something in hearts; after all, a take-out double of one major implies at least tolerance for the unbid major (or a really big hand). The fact that South apparently prefers hearts also limits partner's potential length in the suit. Usually in this sort of sequence, partner has more of a double of spades than he does of hearts. Your hand is some way from the typical 1-4-4-4 he might envisage. With your long strong club suit, you can offer far more playing strength than partner would anticipate and, holding three mediocre hearts, less in the way of defensive values. Relying on partner for something in each major, you should jump to 3NT. The cold vulnerable game proves rather more lucrative than a paltry 300 from defending Two Hearts doubled. ***Do not pass partner's penalty doubles when you can make a higher scoring contract.***

Love All
Dealer East

```
                  ♠ 9 7 4 2
                  ♡ J 9 5
                  ◇ K J 10 5
                  ♣ 8 3
   ♠ Q J 5                        ♠ A K 10 8 6
   ♡ 8 6 4 3           N          ♡ K 7
   ◇ 7 2          W         E     ◇ 9 8 6 4
   ♣ A K 10 4          S          ♣ Q 6
                  ♠ 3
                  ♡ A Q 10 2
                  ◇ A Q 3
                  ♣ J 9 7 5 2
```

YOU	LHO	PARTNER	RHO
–	–	1♠	Double
Redouble	2◇	Double	Pass
?			

As we said at the start of the chapter, a redouble of an opponent's take-out double often indicates penalty ambitions. This means that opener can quite freely double anything the fourth player bids. He will double on any four-card holding and, if he likes the look of his hand defensively, he can do so with only three trumps.

On this hand, you redoubled without any particular aspirations to catch your opponents. You just had the wrong combination of shape and values to raise spades. Two Spades would indicate a weaker hand, and Three Spades would promise four-card support whether or not you play five-card majors. Likewise, you could not jump to 2NT to show a value raise without four. The generally accepted solution is to redouble and, unless something dramatic happens, follow up with Two Spades. This allows you to express your support for partner's suit and your overall strength whilst keeping the bidding low.

As the cards lie, Two Diamonds Doubled is cold. Even if declarer misplayed and went down, you could still score badly. Playing pairs, if the field scores 140 your way, 100 may result in a near bottom. ***Do not pass partner's penalty doubles when you have much weaker defensive values than you might.***

Love All
Dealer North

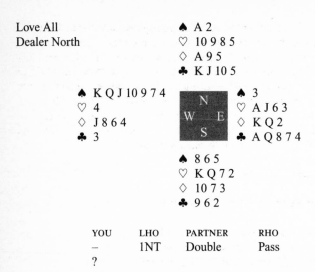

```
                        ♠ A 2
                        ♡ 10 9 8 5
                        ◇ A 9 5
                        ♣ K J 10 5
   ♠ K Q J 10 9 7 4              ♠ 3
   ♡ 4              N             ♡ A J 6 3
   ◇ J 8 6 4    W     E          ◇ K Q 2
   ♣ 3              S             ♣ A Q 8 7 4
                        ♠ 8 6 5
                        ♡ K Q 7 2
                        ◇ 10 7 3
                        ♣ 9 6 2
```

YOU	LHO	PARTNER	RHO
–	1NT	Double	Pass
?			

At times bridge can seem a funny game. A few pages back we told you to leave in partner's double of One No-Trump when your hand offered little or no scope for contributing a trick. Now, when you might take six (if partner has A-x of spades), we say you should take it out!

For a start, things may well turn out badly on the defensive front. RHO's decision to leave the double in on what you guess must be a weak hand tells you he lacks a five-card suit. With both opponents balanced and seven spades in your hand, how many spades do you place partner with? Most likely, he has a singleton. Do you honestly expect him to lead it? Even if he avoids giving away a trick elsewhere and works out you want a spade switch, how do you propose to get back in to run the suit once the ace has gone? On a bad day, 1NT Doubled will make on a minority of values, as it would here.

Conversely, prospects look bright for a Four Spade contract. Partner's high cards will cover some of your losers and any finesses through the 1NT bidder should work. As it happens, with partner's aces helpfully facing your pair of singletons, you can actually make eleven tricks with spades as trumps – five more than you would in no-trumps. This represents a monumental improvement. ***Do not pass partner's penalty doubles when your hand contains very unexpected shape***.

At the risk of stating the obvious, perhaps we had better finish by reminding you that in the chapter's title we carefully preceded the word 'double' with the word 'penalty'. This way we exclude take-out doubles, which you should normally take out. If you leave one of those in, you are effectively making a penalty double yourself, in which case the rules in chapters 11 and 12 apply. Doubles of an artificial bid such as a transfer or a cue bid for the lead do, however, count as penalty doubles: they show the suit bid, imply little interest in other suits, and allow for the possibility that the auction might end.

Golden Rule Thirteen:

Passing Partner's Penalty Doubles can

. . . Allow you to collect a useful penalty;
. . . Avoid turning a plus into a minus;
. . . Save you from conceding a large number;
. . . Give you the chance of a bonanza.

Do not Pass Partner's Penalty Doubles when

. . . You can make a higher scoring contract;
. . . You have much weaker defensive values than you might;
. . . Your hand contains very unexpected shape.

Rule Fourteen: Stand Opponent's Doubles

When someone doubles you or your partner, first instincts may lead you to panic. You might reckon that if trouble looms in your current contract then there just has to be a better spot elsewhere. In practice, you often do best to stay firmly put. Any escape risks taking you out of the frying pan and into the fire. It is even more galling if you start looking fruitlessly for a safer spot and it turns out that the doubler's partner was planning to pull the double anyway.

Game All
Dealer South

♠ K Q 9 6 4
♡ K 10 9 3 2
◇ 7 4
♣ 6

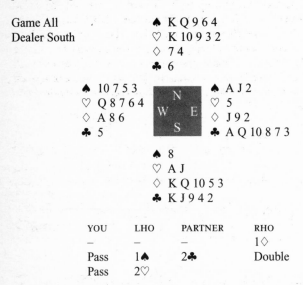

♠ 10 7 5 3
♡ Q 8 7 6 4
◇ A 8 6
♣ 5

♠ A J 2
♡ 5
◇ J 9 2
♣ A Q 10 8 7 3

♠ 8
♡ A J
◇ K Q 10 5 3
♣ K J 9 4 2

YOU	LHO	PARTNER	RHO
–	–	–	1◇
Pass	1♠	2♣	Double
Pass	2♡		

In this day and age, many people would play South's double as competitive or as showing three-card spade support, but assume it is for penalties. With this West collection you have no right to introduce your hearts when South doubles. Partner should hold decent clubs to overcall at the two level when vulnerable and he could have made a take-out double with heart support. Besides, North may be planning to remove the double – if his hand contains diamond support, long spades or, as here, a heart suit. ***Standing opponent's doubles can allow for the fact that the other opponent might take it out***.

♠ 10 6 4   ♠ A 7 3
♡ 6   ♡ Q J 10 9 8 2
◇ K 8 3   ◇ A J 2
♣ Q 10 8 6 4 2   ♣ 3

YOU	LHO	PARTNER	RHO
–	1♠	2♡	Pass
Pass	Double	Pass	Pass
?			

This time you possess a sixth card in your suit and it seems less certain that partner will turn up with six cards in his, but again you should keep quiet about your length. For one thing, LHO may well hold some clubs; he was clearly prepared for RHO to take out the double to Three Clubs. For another, playing in clubs would mean raising the auction to the three level. This means clubs would have to play one trick better than hearts merely to break even. To come away with a profit you would need to score two more tricks. *Standing opponent's doubles can avoid raising the level.*

♠ A 9 6 4 3 2   ♠ 7
♡ J 7 6 2   ♡ 4
◇ –   ◇ K J 10 9 7 6 3
♣ K J 3   ♣ Q 10 6 4

YOU	LHO	PARTNER	RHO
–	1♡	3◇	Pass
Pass	Double	Pass	Pass
?			

For the third example, we have reduced your holding to a void in partner's suit; once more, you must just put down dummy. On this occasion, partner's jump overcall denotes considerable length in diamonds; for a vulnerable weak jump overcall you would hope for a seven-card suit. Sometimes, as here, he will turn up with additional distribution in the shape of a couple of singletons. Indeed, unless the defenders find a club ruff or a trump promotion, Three Diamonds offers some chance of making. *Standing opponent's doubles can cater for extra shape in partner's hand.*

♠ 10 7 3   ♠ A J 4
♡ 10 4 2   ♡ K Q J 7
◇ Q 7 6 5   ◇ J 3
♣ J 8 3   ♣ Q 10 7 4

YOU	LHO	PARTNER	RHO
–	–	1NT	Double
?			

Some people say that the art of surviving when someone doubles a 1NT opener depends on having a good rescue system. We feel inclined to dispute this. Lacking a five-card suit, you often do better to take the medicine at the one level. Any escape move carries you to the two level and comes with no assurance of landing in a four-four fit. The advice to stand your ground holds still more strongly with a completely flat hand. Very rarely can you score the two extra tricks needed to make raising the level show a clear gain. With these hands together, you might score the same six tricks in no-trumps, clubs or hearts. *Standing opponent's doubles can cut your losses*.

♠ K J 7 3   ♠ 8 4 2
♡ A 8 6   ♡ 10 7
◇ A K J 7   ◇ 6
♣ 6 5   ♣ A Q 10 9 8 7 2

YOU	LHO	PARTNER	RHO
–	1♡	3♣	Pass
3NT	Pass	Pass	Double
?			

Despite holding a 16-count, potting 3NT after partner's weak jump overcall was by no means clear-cut. You have only one heart stopper and little help in clubs. For sure, when RHO wields the axe, this has to be a case of discreetly beating a hasty retreat. Unless LHO turns up with ♣K-x (unlikely as RHO should have club values to double), the suit will not run and you could go a lot down. Four Clubs may well make (losing two spades and a club) and would be unlucky to fail by more than a trick. Besides, it might escape being doubled. *Do not stand opponent's doubles when the risk is too high*.

♠ 8 7	♠ K Q 6 5 2
♡ 10 6 4	♡ A Q 2
◇ J 10 9 8 6 2	◇ K 4
♣ 7 3	♣ A J 2

YOU	LHO	PARTNER	RHO
–	–	1♠	Pass
Pass	Double	1NT	Double
?			

This situation differs from those seen so far. This time partner has shown a good hand – he ought to hold better than a strong no-trump opening, i.e., 18-19 points. Still, unless his values include ◇A-K-x, your hand offers little as dummy – and even then someone could turn up with Q-x-x. It must make more sense to try to play in diamonds. Moreover, you can feel hopeful about finding at least tolerance for the suit in partner's hand. Holding a singleton anywhere, surely he would have redoubled or called a second suit. *Do not stand opponent's doubles when you are confident of finding a better spot.*

♠ 9 6 2	♠ J 7 4
♡ Q 9 6 4 2	♡ K 10 3
◇ 10 7 3	◇ A K Q 4
♣ Q 4	♣ 7 6 2

YOU	LHO	PARTNER	RHO
–	–	1NT	Double
?			

Playing a weak (12-14) no-trump, you sense danger when RHO pulls out the red card. Do you run? On this hand, you cannot be sure to score more tricks with hearts as trumps. For one thing, partner could have two small hearts. For another, your doubleton club queen appears more likely to play a part in a no-trump contract. However, there is one excellent reason for running. Two Hearts doubled, if made, scores game. Most opponents shy away from doubling you into game. They know that if you hold six hearts or a bit of shape, you might scramble eight tricks with the minority of values. *Do not stand opponent's doubles when your run-out may not be doubled.*

East–West game

Dealer East

♠ K J 10 8 6 5
♡ 7 6
♢ A 7 5 2
♣ 6

♠ A 9
♡ A K J 10 8 5 3
♢ J 10 6
♣ 4

♠ Q 7 3 2
♡ 9
♢ Q 8
♣ A Q J 8 5 3

♠ 4
♡ Q 4 2
♢ K 9 4 3
♣ K 10 9 7 2

YOU	LHO	PARTNER	RHO
–	–	1♣	Pass
1♡	1♠	2♣	Double
?			

With your hand, you feel optimistic about the heart game when you hear partner open the bidding. You can see seven tricks – eight if your diamond combination produces a trick or you can pick up the trumps without loss. Surely partner's opening bid will include enough to score the remainder. Does the chance to play in Two Clubs doubled alter anything? If it is passed out, partner can just scrape home. He wins the spade in dummy, crosses to the ♣A, finesses the ♡J and runs hearts until South ruffs. Of course, this may not happen: North holds a hand on which he might have made a weak jump overcall if he had one available and he will probably remove the double.

The trouble here is that because minors only score 20 points a trick, Two Clubs doubled does not give you game. Two real choices present themselves: simply to bid Four Hearts, or to go looking for a possible 3NT contract. The former sounds best to us.

Finally, what do you think of South's double? We judge him guilty of looking for a penalty prematurely. Despite holding five trumps sitting over declarer, he is never going to get rich at the two level. If your side really is heading for trouble, he should wait for you to get higher rather than start doubling and warning you of the potential danger. *Do not stand opponent's doubles when you can make a higher-scoring contract elsewhere.*

♠ A J 10 9 3		♠ K Q 4 2	
♡ K 8 6		♡ Q	
◇ A K J		◇ 10 5	
♣ 5 3		♣ A K J 10 8 6	

YOU	LHO	PARTNER	RHO
–	–	1♣	Pass
1♠	Pass	3♡ *	Pass
4NT *	Pass	5♠ *	Pass
6♠	Pass	Pass	Double
?			

With the aid of a 3♡ mini Splinter (showing spade support with precisely one heart) and Roman Key-Card Blackwood, you sail into what looks like the best contract, Six Spades. This all changes when South doubles. No doubt he holds a void in clubs and, with the ace of hearts almost certainly missing, you will lose the first two or three tricks. It seems much better to take your chances in 6NT. You have the king of hearts as a stopper and, knowing that any club finesses will work, you can reasonably hope for twelve tricks in no-trumps. ***Do not stand opponent's doubles when you fear a ruff.***

Golden Rule Fourteen:

Standing Opponent's Doubles can

. . . Allow for the fact that the other opponent might take it out;
. . . Avoid raising the level;
. . . Cater for extra shape in partner's hand;
. . . Cut your losses.

Do not Stand Opponent's Doubles when

. . . The risk is too high;
. . . You are confident of finding a better spot;
. . . Your run-out may not be doubled;
. . . You can make a higher-scoring contract elsewhere;
. . . You fear a ruff.

Rule Fifteen: Never Redouble

There are plenty of card games amply suited to gamblers, poker and blackjack for example, but bridge is not one of them. Its high-stake action, the redouble, exists as the ultimate sanction to deter frivolous doubles; you should use it sparingly. A good player who doubles probably has a surprise in store for you. Never assume otherwise.

Redoubles can win or, more likely, lose matches. In the 1998-9 Tollemache Cup (for inter-county teams of 8) the eventual winners (Hampshire & Isle of Wight) were in danger of not getting to the final. However, a 2200 penalty that one pair collected from 1NT redoubled on an innocuous-looking deal on which the high cards split 20-20 revived their flagging fortunes. Let this serve as a lesson to all.

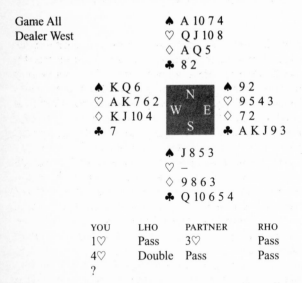

Game All
Dealer West

North:
♠ A 10 7 4
♡ Q J 10 8
◇ A Q 5
♣ 8 2

West:
♠ K Q 6
♡ A K 7 6 2
◇ K J 10 4
♣ 7

East:
♠ 9 2
♡ 9 5 4 3
◇ 7 2
♣ A K J 9 3

South:
♠ J 8 5 3
♡ –
◇ 9 8 6 3
♣ Q 10 6 5 4

YOU	LHO	PARTNER	RHO
1♡	Pass	3♡	Pass
4♡	Double	Pass	Pass
?			

Whether you count losers or high cards, you certainly hold a better hand than you needed to for raising to game. Even so, it would be a mistake to redouble. Remember, if North goes by our advice, he has hopes of beating you by two tricks, and he is right. True, you hardly like losing 500, but the other table may flatten the result and –1000 is far worse. ***Never redoubling can keep down possible losses.***

Game All
Dealer West

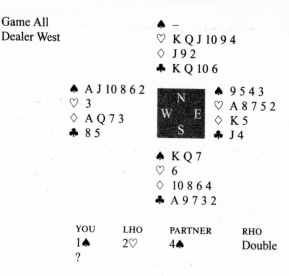

```
                        ♠ –
                        ♡ K Q J 10 9 4
                        ◇ J 9 2
                        ♣ K Q 10 6
    ♠ A J 10 8 6 2           N           ♠ 9 5 4 3
    ♡ 3                                   ♡ A 8 7 5 2
    ◇ A Q 7 3         W           E       ◇ K 5
    ♣ 8 5                  S               ♣ J 4
                        ♠ K Q 7
                        ♡ 6
                        ◇ 10 8 6 4
                        ♣ A 9 7 3 2
```

YOU	LHO	PARTNER	RHO
1♠	2♡	4♠	Double
?			

A double can be a solo action by one opponent, something his partner may feel rather unhappy about. As we discussed in chapter 13, North will usually elect to defend when South doubles, but he may reconsider the matter if you redouble. Adding your hand to the values shown by South's double, you can easily conclude that North has overcalled on a distributional hand. If you give him an excuse to remove the double, he may well take it. Okay, your partner could turn up with a heart stack and be ready to deal with any rescue move. However, you can see no reason to believe this applies here. In any case, North might hold a second suit. Partner will always have four trumps for his leap to game and will often put down five. If your side owns a 10- or 11-card spade fit, the opponents must have a good fit somewhere. On the actual layout, North can get out for down two in Five Clubs. This will give you 500 if you correctly judge to double and to avoid bidding 5 Spades (okay – not so tough).

Your sixth spade, strong trump intermediates, prime cards in diamonds and extra shape all suggest you stand every chance of making Four Spades Doubled. If, as you suspect, the opponents have misjudged – or if they are on a different wavelength about what South's action means – you will get a good score merely for making ten tricks in your doubled contract. *Never redoubling can avoid scaring opponents into finding a cheap sacrifice.*

Love All
Dealer South

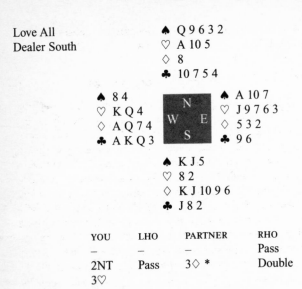

```
                  ♠ Q 9 6 3 2
                  ♡ A 10 5
                  ◇ 8
                  ♣ 10 7 5 4
     ♠ 8 4                        ♠ A 10 7
     ♡ K Q 4            N         ♡ J 9 7 6 3
     ◇ A Q 7 4     W         E    ◇ 5 3 2
     ♣ A K Q 3          S         ♣ 9 6
                  ♠ K J 5
                  ♡ 8 2
                  ◇ K J 10 9 6
                  ♣ J 8 2
```

YOU	LHO	PARTNER	RHO
–	–	–	Pass
2NT	Pass	3◇ *	Double
3♡			

On this deal, you announce a balanced 20-22 and partner initiates a transfer. He may hold a weak hand and intend to sign off in Three Hearts, or he may wish to make a slam try, but most likely he is looking for the best game. Because of the transfer, South expects his partner to be on lead against either a heart or no-trump contract, so he has doubled to request an opening diamond lead. Since he cannot tell what type of contract you are going to end up in, he needs both length and strength in diamonds to show a profit. Of course, to ensure he cannot treat this as a cost-nothing option, you will want on occasion to teach him a lesson by redoubling Three Diamonds.

To redouble you must hold four diamonds, although five is better, and you need to consider your intermediates. Here your diamond spots fall short of the ideal. Moreover, your secondary heart values look better offensively. All in all, it seems much more prudent to show your support by completing the transfer with 3♡ (you would pass without support). Partner will easily raise to the cold game. If instead you pulled out a blue card, he would take one look at his three diamonds and pass. He would go a disastrous one down in Three Diamonds Redoubled and a happy partnership could end. *Never redoubling can allow you to go for a likely game elsewhere*.

	YOU	LHO	PARTNER	RHO
♠ 8 4	YOU	LHO	PARTNER	RHO
♡ A Q 8 6	–	–	1♠	Double
◇ 4	?			
♣ A K J 9 7 4				

We must temper slightly our advice never to redouble when the opposing double asks for take-out. In this situation, you scarcely expect the contract to be passed out. This means that a redouble takes on a special meaning, typically good values, and sometimes a desire to penalize the opponents. For many years, it was standard practice to redouble on any hand with 11+ points when RHO doubles partner's opening bid. The snag occurs if LHO has a shapely hand and can safely pre-empt. If you were to redouble and hear LHO bounce to Three Diamonds, you would be in a mess. It works out much better to play a change of suit as forcing as then you can start with Two Clubs. You can reverse into hearts next time and this should put you well on the way to finding the best contract. *Never redoubling can enable you to start a constructive sequence.*

	YOU	LHO	PARTNER	RHO
♠ 6	YOU	LHO	PARTNER	RHO
♡ Q J 9 7	–	–	1♠	Double
◇ K 10 7 6	?			
♣ A J 6 5				

As we saw on the last hand, it is often sensible to make the same bid as you would without the double. Naturally, exceptions can arise. Situations on which it works best to start with a redouble include when you have a balanced 10-12 points either with or without 3-card support for partner. In both cases you cannot bid 2NT as that would promise 4-card support. You can safely redouble knowing you will get another bid (indeed you promise another bid; this way partner can pass if LHO acts). However, the classic hand for the redouble looks like this, where you hold the other three suits and want to punish RHO for his entry into the auction. Your redouble creates a forcing situation; it invites partner to double if LHO bids or, unless he has an unbalanced minimum, to wait to see if you can double. *Redouble when their double is for take-out and you want to defend.*

	YOU	LHO	PARTNER	RHO
♠ K 6		1◇	1♠	Double
♡ 10 6 4	–			
◇ Q 9 6 5 2	?			
♣ 10 8 7				

Before you act on this auction, you must first check, if you do not already know from LHO's alert or failure to alert, what RHO's double means. If it is a penalty double, just sit tight. Conversely, if, as most pairs do nowadays, your opponents play it is as a negative double suggesting four hearts and some high cards, you should redouble. This cannot logically mean that you hold a good hand; their actions limit your values. Rather it promises the ace or king of spades and asks partner to lead a spade if he has the opening lead – quite likely as LHO may become declarer in any denomination except spades.

Some authorities (the Rosenkranz school) allow the redouble to be made with the ace, king or queen, but we regard this as unsound. If you hold the queen and LHO the king, do you really want partner leading from his ace against a suit contract? Note also that the redouble denies primary support. With enough spades to raise, you should ignore the double and make your normal bid. *Redouble when the double is negative and you would like the suit led*.

	YOU	LHO	PARTNER	RHO
♠ A Q 8 7 4	1♠	Pass	4♣	Double
♡ Q 10 2				
◇ Q 6	?			
♣ A 8 4				

Partner's Splinter promises a singleton (or void) club, so your redouble ought to mean the ace. Other types of control will hardly interest partner and there is no question of playing in clubs. Indeed, if you cue-bid four of a red suit here, partner will assume you cannot have the club ace. On a different day you might pass the double (to deny the club ace), in which case redouble from partner would also show first-round control – probably a void – possibly the bare ace.

Note that if ever you make a cue bid showing first-round control of a suit and they double, a redouble by you or partner should indicate second-round control. In that situation this is likely to be the most helpful information. *Redouble when you have the right control on a possible slam hand*.

East–West game
Dealer East

	♠ K J 10 8 5
	♡ A Q 2
	♢ 7 4
	♣ Q 4 3

♠ A Q 9 3
♡ J 10 6
♢ A 8 3
♣ K J 6

♠ 4
♡ K 8 4 3
♢ K Q 10 6 5
♣ A 9 5

♠ 7 6 2
♡ 9 7 5
♢ J 9 2
♣ 10 8 7 2

YOU	LHO	PARTNER	RHO
–	–	1♢	Pass
1♠	Pass	1NT	Pass
3NT	Double	Pass	Pass
?			

On the first three 'rule-breaking' examples about redoubling, you had little or no intention of playing the redoubled contract. Still, on rare occasions, you will have the chance to rake in the money with a business redouble This seems most likely to happen when your opponent makes a lead-directing double of your contract. The odds make Lightner-style doubles much more attractive than doubles that carry no lead-directing connotation, so people will sometimes make speculative doubles of this nature. Since they are generally going to score well if their side has the goods to defeat the contract on the right lead, you will need to make the most of situations like this when their luck is out. No matter what the range of partner's 1NT rebid, your 15-count indicates that you can underwrite the values for game even taking account of possible bad breaks and a losing spade finesse. Your nine of spades could also prove a key card, since you know that RHO would need to lead spades several times to prevent your spade holding from amounting to a double stopper.

As the cards lie, partner takes ten easy tricks. With the redoubled overtrick counting as 400 points, increasing the stakes is well worth doing. ***Redouble when you have a big surprise for the doubler.***

Game All   ♠ K 9 4
Dealer North   ♡ A K 7 6 5 2
              ◇ 8 4 2
              ♣ 8

    ♠ Q J 6   ♠ 10 3 2
    ♡ Q J 10 8   ♡ 3
    ◇ A K 10   ◇ 7 5
    ♣ A 7 6   ♣ K Q 10 9 5 4 2

              ♠ A 8 7 5
              ♡ 9 4
              ◇ Q J 9 6 3
              ♣ J 3

YOU	LHO	PARTNER	RHO
–	1♡	3♣	Pass
3NT	Pass	Pass	Double
?			

As we discussed in chapter 14, normally you stand your ground when an opponent doubles your contract. This means that you rarely need to redouble to deter partner from bailing out. Even so, there are times when one of you might take a gamble to secure a game bonus, a gamble you would see through in normal circumstances, but not when you risk losing a large penalty. With no club ace and lacking an outside entry or help to stop either of the enemy suits, partner may well worry about the danger of going down a lot in 3NT doubled. To reassure him, you should redouble. You should understand that a desire to increase the score provides only a secondary motivation for the redouble. The main one is to say 'Even if you have a minimum for your bid, I am confident of making the contract. Please do not run.'

Of course, if you were in the pass out seat, the above argument would cease to apply. You could use the redouble in the traditional way, seeking to punish the opposition for an injudicious double, but many pairs use it in this position to express doubt. If you were content, you would simply settle for the doubled contract. You will need to discuss with your partner which way round you play a redouble in this alternative situation. *Redouble when partner might mistakenly run if you fail to do so*.

North–South game
Dealer East

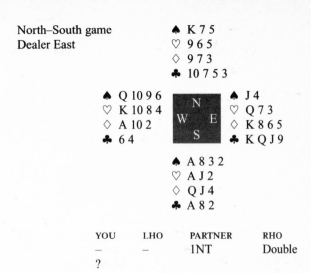

```
                        ♠ K 7 5
                        ♡ 9 6 5
                        ◇ 9 7 3
                        ♣ 10 7 5 3

  ♠ Q 10 9 6                         ♠ J 4
  ♡ K 10 8 4         N               ♡ Q 7 3
  ◇ A 10 2      W         E          ◇ K 8 6 5
  ♣ 6 4              S               ♣ K Q J 9

                        ♠ A 8 3 2
                        ♡ A J 2
                        ◇ Q J 4
                        ♣ A 8 2
```

YOU	LHO	PARTNER	RHO
–	–	1NT	Double
?			

Despite what we said in the chapter's introduction, you are more likely to redouble 1NT than any other contract. People will double a 1NT opener with a better hand than the opening bidder (i.e., 15 plus if 1NT shows 12-14). They hope their partner possesses a fair share of the missing values, in which case their side will own the balance of power. On occasion, you can tell as responder that your opponent's luck is out. The fact that 1NT doubled cannot score game, but that 1NT redoubled can, makes a redouble more attractive than usual. Also, knowing where the opposing strength lies can counterbalance whatever advantage the enemy may derive from the opening lead.

As always, you need to consider whether the opposition might have somewhere to escape to safely. You must also take account of the danger that the doubler turns up with a running suit. So, strange though it may seem, it can prove safer to redouble with nine points than fourteen – too many high cards should warn you of the long suit possibility. On the actual layout, the opponents can do nothing to harm you. If they elect to defend One No-Trump Redoubled, partner will make two overtricks. If they run, you can extract an 800 penalty from doubling either Two Clubs or their eventual retreat to Two Spades. Your redouble announces that your side has the balance of power and invites partner to apply the axe if they run. ***Redouble when you expect to turn the contract into a sound game.***

	YOU	LHO	PARTNER	RHO
♠ 6 4		1♠	2♣	Pass
♡ J 10 9 8 6	–	1♠	2♣	Pass
◇ Q 10 9 6 4 3	Pass	Double	Pass	Pass
♣ –	?			

The rarity of the business redouble makes it sensible in certain auctions to assign a different meaning to the call, as specifically asking for rescue. Originally named the Koch-Werner redouble after its Swedish inventors, most people now know it as an SOS redouble.

On the hand here, you can judge that Two Clubs Doubled is not your optimum spot. Rather than guess which red suit to play in, consult partner with a redouble. With equal length, he will tend to prefer the lower suit, diamonds, so you will hardly ever end up in an inferior contract. It goes without saying that your partner never passes this redouble – unless he has eight certain tricks in his hand! *Redouble when it asks for rescue*.

Golden Rule Fifteen:

Never Redoubling can

. . . Keep down possible losses;
. . . Avoid scaring opponents into finding a cheap sacrifice;
. . . Allow you to go for a likely game elsewhere;
. . . Enable you to start a constructive sequence.

Redouble when

. . . Their double is for a take-out and you want to defend;
. . . The double is negative and you would like the suit led;
. . . You have the right control on a possible slam hand;
. . . You have a big surprise for the doubler;
. . . Partner might mistakenly run if you fail to do so;
. . . You expect to turn the contract into a sound game;
. . . It asks for rescue (Koch-Werner or SOS convention).